Dirks Escape

C. BRANDON RIMMER

**The true story
of a German family
fleeing from the specter
of the holocaust**

Rachel + Wil:
   Happy Thanksgiving!
I thought you'd enjoy
reading this, since I
mentioned it recently.
         Love,
            Doris

H Bethany Fellowship INC.
MINNEAPOLIS, MINNESOTA 55438

The Dirks Escape
C. Brandon Rimmer

ISBN 0-87123-108-5

Copyright © 1978
Bethany Fellowship, Inc.
All Rights Reserved

DIMENSION BOOKS
Published by Bethany Fellowship, Inc.
6820 Auto Club Road, Minneapolis, Minnesota 55438

Printed in the United States of America

Dedicated to our own R2D2

Introduction

This is the unforgettable story of a man running for his life—Herr Doktor Gerhard Dirks. There were many who were after him, the Nazis and the S.S., the Communists and the Volkpolizei. He made it to freedom in the West because of his courage and his brains.

Although he didn't know it at the time, Dirks knows now that he had something even more important than courage and brains. He had God's help in escaping the many dangers he encountered.

When Dirks came to the West, he brought a lot with him. His inventions have been pivotal in the development of the computer. In the minds of some people who are familiar with both American and European computer history, Dirks is the father of the modern computer. Where computers have touched our lives (and who can count the places?) he has touched them. In order that the reader may know that this is no exaggeration, there is a list of the positions and some inventions of this incredibly productive man in an appendix at the close of the book.

Today, Dr. Dirks lives in Northern California. As a citizen of the United States and a knowledgeable observer of our society, he points out some dangers about the present drift of our country—a country he has learned to love. These observations, based on the life he once led in East Germany as an atheist and the life he leads today as an American Christian, are printed in italics at the ends of three chapters.

Gerhard Dirks, in the time span covered by this book, made three remarkable escapes: from Naziism, from Communism, and from atheism.

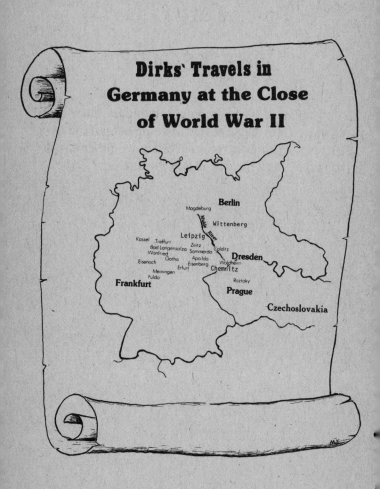

Dirks' Travels in Germany at the Close of World War II

Berlin

Magdeburg

Mulde River

Wittenberg

Leipzig

Kassel Treffurt

Zeitz Colditz

Bad Langensalza Sommerda

Wanfried

Dresden

Eisenach Gotha Apolda Eisenberg Waldheim

Erfurt Chemnitz

Meiningen

Fulda

Roztoky

Frankfurt

Prague

Czechoslovakia

M.V.

Part I

THE ESCAPE

Names of some people and places have been changed to protect those still living behind the Iron Curtain. Wherever total accuracy would endanger someone, facts have been slightly altered.

ONE

For the first time in his adult life, Herr Doktor Gerhard Dirks felt fear—cold, clammy and right in the pit of his stomach. Every German wanted to leave Prague, Czechoslovakia, because the Russians were coming. Stories drifting back from territory that the Communists had already captured would put terror in any human heart. The fear never left him. It was in the back of his mind no matter what else he was thinking about, and it was always accompanied by the question, "How do I get myself and my family away from the Communists?" A thousand schemes had gone through his head and been rejected, but a plan had taken shape, a plan that might work. Step by step, he had started to implement it.

He turned his head and looked out the window of the train that was taking him from his "gardenhouse" home in the suburb city of Roztoky to his office in downtown Prague. The dirty train window acted as a mirror, and in it he could see the conductor working his way through the car checking tickets. There were no police with the conductor, for the train was a commuter and could provide no way of escape. Had the train been a north-bound express, the conductor and the train police would have been going over every passenger's papers with the greatest of care.

The conductor reached Gerhard and punched the proffered ticket. The man was a Czech and he spoke to Dirks in a cool way, but with respect. Coolly, because Dirks was German, and with respect because he knew Dirks' position at the huge international firm of Skodaserk AG.

Dirks was line controller for all the Skoda factories. Skoda had 65,000 employees in steel mills, foundries, and in factories manufacturing machinery, electro-machinery, cars, tanks, artillery, airplanes, locomotives—and much of it was controlled by a process that Gerhard Dirks had developed. The entire data processing procedure used 3,000,000 punch cards every month. In addition to this production control punch card system, he had established the new cost accounting and cost control systems implemented in all Skoda plants. It had taken time. He'd first visited Skoda in Prague, going there from Berlin to consult and to direct, but when Berlin had been bombed and when the parent company offices had been destroyed, he had been transferred to Prague.

Dirks turned back to the window and looked at himself. His double-breasted grey suit had been expensive, his shirt was grey and soft green, and his necktie contained a broad stripe that matched the green in his shirt. He said to himself sarcastically, "Every inch the successful business executive."

Dirks couldn't help feeling bitter. He and thousands like him had worked diligently to build Germany, not really stopping to think about where Germany was ultimately headed. Now their country was coming down around their ears like a pile of useless, twisted junk.

The train pulled into the station at Prague and once more he noted the difference between Prague and Berlin. The stations in Berlin were a shambles. He had been relieved when he had been moved to Prague because he felt his family would get out from under the bombing. He had thought he was pulling them out of danger. Now the danger was reversed. It would have been easier to get west from Berlin than from Prague. He couldn't get them back to Berlin. Leaving the "Protectorate", i.e., conquered country, was treason—punishable by death—for it showed "defeatism." It was quite a trick to get permission to go back into Germany. He might—no, he must—do it.

The train jerked to a halt. Dirks walked through the main exit of the Prague train station. The door was under the building's tower, a tower that displayed the largest clock in a city full of clocks. On top of the station clock, a huge metal eagle with wings spread surveyed the scurrying crowd below. The eagle was a reminder of the days of Austrian occupation. Dirks walked down the Wenzelplatz toward his office still thinking about his plan of escape, mulling it over in his mind yet again, trying to think of alternate solutions to possible complications. Gestapo or no Gestapo, S.S. or no S.S., he was going to get his mother, his wife, his two sons and his daughter to where the Russians couldn't touch them. The first step in the plan he was implementing depended on a Czech doctor, their family physician back in Rostoky. He looked at his watch. It was just time for his wife to be leaving their home and heading for the doctor's office. He hoped things went well.

* * *

Gertrud Dirks was a handsome woman, a straight-backed, well-proportioned blonde. She was more Nordic than her husband, and her three children, blue-eyed blondes with smooth features, had taken after her. She had dressed carefully that morning, preparing for her visit to the doctor's office. Gerhard had told her to go to the doctor, and what to say. She would do it. She had the typical confidence in her husband that went with her class and station in life.

The view from the second story window of their garden house was lovely even in the closing days of winter. There were many evergreens, and what food could be planted so early in the year had been planted in even, straight rows. The garden had been a blessing. Back in Berlin the children had not had all they wanted to eat, and if the baby, Wolfgang, had been born in Berlin, she would have been hard pressed to nurse him. To her immense relief, both hunger and the bombs had ended when they moved to Prague. The garden supplied extra food and there were no raids over the Czech city. The peace had been short-lived. The Russians were coming. Gertrud fought down the feeling of terror. She must be calm at the doctor's office.

The children were being left in the care of her sister-in-law, Irmgest, a woman in her late twenties who lived with the Dirkses and helped with the children. She was as anxious as the rest of the family to get to the west. What the Russians did to German women when they caught them was not pleasant; not all of the women lived through the experience. She watched anxiously as Gertrud left the house through the front door and descended the steps to the street. It was a cold morning and a ten-block walk. Gertrud walked briskly.

The doctor saw her promptly. As they sat in his office, the doctor had a half-smile on his face. He had an idea about what it was Gertrud would ask.

Did the doctor remember that Ingrid and Wolfgang had had the whooping cough? Yes, he remembered prescribing some medicine. Didn't the doctor think it would be good for the children's health if they got away from the city and into the country? The doctor ignored the fact that in the suburb they were living in the country already, and said that he thought it was a fine idea.

"Where can you send your children where they will be well cared for?"

Gertrud hesitated for a moment, as if the idea were just occurring to her. "My mother lives in Bad Langensalza. The children would get the best of care from their grandmother, and the air at

Langensalza should do them a world of good."

The Czech doctor smiled to himself. He wasn't sure where Bad Langensalza was, but he was reasonably sure of one thing—it was west of the Elbe River. Rumor had it that that river was to be the dividing line between the American and the Russian sectors when Germany was divided by the Allies. A man in Dirks' position, a driving and directing force in Skoda's production of war material, would be a man who would want his family in the American sector. The Czech was willing to cooperate as the rumors in his community were that Dirks was easier to get along with than many Germans and was useful to the Czechs. The doctor didn't understand it all, but he believed the rumors and was willing to cooperate.

He pulled his prescription pad out of the desk drawer and put it on the front of his desk, prepared to write. With some humor he asked, "Would you spell the name of that town for me, please?"

Gertrud spelled it.

"Someone will accompany the children?"

"Yes, my sister-in-law Irmgest. She's staying with us."

The physician wrote out the prescription ordering the two children and one adult to Bad Langensalza for reasons of health. The doctor had no doubt that the S.S. would let a man of Dirks' stature send two of his children west for their health on a doctor's orders, particularly when both Dirks and his wife were remaining in Prague.

He handed the prescription to Gertrud. She

thanked him profusely and left. If all went well, there would be three in the west. Three down and four to go.

The next morning, Ingrid and Wolfgang, accompanied by their young aunt, went with Gerhard to Prague on the morning commuter. At the station, they wandered around for a half-hour until it was time to get on their west bound train. Dirks helped them aboard with their luggage and a large basket of food. He stood on the platform until the train left. For the children, it could be a long, tiresome and difficult trip. Train service was not what it had once been, but they were headed in the right direction, west. Gerhard was late for work that morning for the first time in his life.

* * *

It was a month before the expected letter arrived from Bad Langensalza. Gerhard knew what was in the letter before he opened it, as he had composed the original for the family doctor in Langensalza. Gertrud had forwarded it to her mother to give to her doctor and have him copy it into his own handwriting and mail it back to Prague. The original, in Dirks' handwriting, was to be destroyed.

The letter said that the children were not improving in health as had been hoped. Their grandmother would like to keep them, but their grandmother was suffering from—here the doctor described her genuine heart problem in Latin—and she would not be strong enough to care for the two sick children. Someone would have to come get them and take them back to Prague.

When Dirks took the train into Prague the next morning, the letter was in his pocket. It was time to put step two into action. He left the station, walked down the Wenzelplatz wondering how many more times he would be doing so before he got away. He intended to be the last of his family to leave Prague.

He turned right, walked through an arch and into the Skoda Building. Two or three Czech employees passed close to him and spoke respectfully. Gerhard had come to terms with the people at Skoda on a very realistic basis when he had first arrived from Berlin. The Czechs had no love for the Germans, and less for the Nazis. They believed firmly in the eventual defeat of Germany and the arrival of the Allies. The Czechs were looking forward to freedom. They expected the Allies to get the Nazis off their back and return their country to its pre-Nazi status. The idea that at a place called Yalta, Roosevelt would hand them over to Joseph Stalin, didn't even cross their minds.

They were willing to go along with Dirks to learn what they would need to know when they once again controlled their own industry. Because of past ownership and control by the French, the Skoda factories had been under the Schneider-Creuzot systems of accounting and production control. The systems were years behind the times. Dirks could teach them the very latest and most successful methods and procedures. He had a tacit deal with them: "You work for me, and work well, and I will teach you."

In 1944 and early 1945 in Prague, this looked like a very good deal. The Czechs worked for Dirks, did as they were told, and asked intelligent questions while they waited for the German war machine to collapse and the Allies to arrive. It was the hammer and sickle that arrived and it is a matter of historical irony that when that terrible day came little distinction was made between Czech and German. Only Czechs with previous relationships to Russian Communism profited from the holocaust.

Inside the Skoda building, Dirks climbed the stairs to his office on the second floor. His desk was unusual. As far as he knew, it was the only one in the whole Reich with two microphones on it. The microphones led to two dictating machines that were outside of his office. This dictation was transcribed by two very busy secretaries and an assistant. One of the three would have to go to the personnel office for him.

No Czech wanted to go, because the personnel office was the exclusive province of the German S.S., the Storm Troopers. While the S.S. personnel at Skoda were more clerical than combatant, they were nonetheless S.S. and few people cared to be around them if the contact could be avoided. No Skoda employee was hired, fired or transferred without the knowledge and consent of the S.S. In-

deed, absolutely no one connected with Skoda had
any chance of crossing the border back into Germany without carrying their written permission.
Dirks' sister-in-law and two small, sick children
had been passed through, but Gerhard himself
would have to have more than their implied consent.

One of the two secretaries was an older, heavier
woman with a reasonably calm disposition. It
would probably be easier for her to talk to the S.S.
than the others. Gerhard called her into his office.
She came, pencil and pad in hand, expecting more
dictation.

Rather than dictating, Dirks reached into his
inside coat pocket and pulled out the letter from
the doctor in Langensalza. He handed it to her as
he spoke.

"It is apparent that my children are not doing
well; they are still sickly. Their grandmother is no
longer able to care for them. I want you to go to
the personnel office and get travel permits for me.
My wife, Gertrud, and I will go get the children
and bring them back. We will have to take our son
Rainer with us. My mother is here in Prague, but
she cannot care for the boy. Her knees are swollen
and she can walk only a little." That part was true
enough. "Get permission for three people to go to
Bad Langensalza and for five to return."

He had conveniently forgotten to mention the
children's young aunt, and he hoped the S.S.
wouldn't remember her. There was no reason to

think they would unless someone had called attention to her departure. When she had left she had had no intention of ever coming back to Prague.

The secretary nodded and left to go to the personnel office. Dirks watched her go and thought the plan through yet again. The letter from Langensalza was genuine and the postmark readable. His request was for a round trip. His own mother would be in Prague as a hostage against his return. He could think of nothing that would rouse the S.S. suspicions, except that they were the S.S. and were always suspicious. He sat down at his desk and tried to work, but the sweat running down the small of his back was distracting. The woman was gone for half an hour, the longest thirty minutes in Dirks' life to that date.

She came back into his office with a hand full of papers. "Here you are, Dr. Dirks."

He didn't trust himself to reach for the papers; his hand would shake. "Thank you, just put them on my desk."

She did so, turned and walked away.

TWO

Gerhard's work at Skoda would have been more than enough for any normal man—the pressures were very heavy. But to him, his position at Skoda was only one of two jobs, and his heart was in the second. He had an electronics laboratory near his home in Roztoky.

The lab was under the auspices of what had once been an English company, Power's Business Machines. That company had done well in Germany until the war started. After the outbreak of hostilities, Power's had been taken over by a German firm, and taken over intact. Although Gerhard had never worked for Power's directly, he had done things for them on the outside. After the takeover, he had kept his contacts with the firm. This was important at the time, and would be important later. When the war was over, much of the company was returned to Power's. In time they were absorbed by the American firm, Remington Rand.

It was in the lab at Roztoky that three strands of Dirks' life were woven into one effort.

He had received a Doctor of Laws from the University of Leipzig, but more important to his career, he had also received a masters of business administration from the business school. With his degrees in hand he had taken his first position. A group of German paper mills hired him and put him in the accounting department. It was there that he had used one of the first bookkeeping machines ever built.

He soon understood how the machine worked and began to get things out of it that no one else knew were there. This ability, combined with his insight into accounting problems, caused him to rise rapidly within the firms. He was soon in charge of general accounting, cost accounting and production projections. Because of this experience he grasped firmly an important concept: business machines could be very valuable. He began to be interested in them and their development. It was an interest that grew until it was a consuming drive which stayed with him all the rest of his life. He knew the worth of business machine development from the point of view of the end user.

He also knew, intuitively and by experience, electro-mechanics. He had grown up in his father's shop in Magdaburg and later in his father's factory in Leipzig. Dirks senior had battled to keep his factory open. In the end, material shortages, poor delivery and rampant inflation had closed it. The factory had manufactured electrical and mechanical parts that were used to control printing machines. By the time Gerhard was ten years old, he spent his after school hours sitting at one of his father's benches assembling and soldering.

It wasn't only switches that he soldered. Radio was new and fascinated him. He was soon building, then designing and building his own sets. Techniques thus acquired contributed to his ability to build the first model of a device that could assess data for transmitting over telephone and teletype lines, and do it at what was then a very high rate of speed. It was this device, built at Roztoky, that was to give him useful contacts with influential people at the close of the war. This same combination of abilities enabled him to build the first business computer. He finished it in Frankfurt in 1953 and it is in the IBM museum near Stuttgart.

Dirks had electro-mechanical know how, he had electro-mechanical theory, he knew the problems of business data processing and communications and was aware of the immense value of their solutions. So, when he had been moved to Prague from Berlin, he had sent for his father and together they had built their lab at Roztoky. In it he was able to turn his dreams into something tangible. But after only a year, the senior Dirks fell ill and died. The whole burden of the lab became Gerhard's.

Not only did he get the burden, he got the privileges. There was a silver lining. Any material he wanted or needed for the lab would be provided for him on request, if it was available anywhere in the Reich. The military's need for rapid data access and communications had grown desperate.

Hitler had entered a war for which he was not prepared—the war against Russia. The German

Army was now stranded at Moscow and unless materials could reach that front, it would soon collapse. Two things were needed. First, information as to the exact nature of the most critical shortages. Second, and equally important, how was the required material to be delivered? There was a growing shortage of everything needed to deliver anything. Much equipment had been destroyed. Skoda was building rapidly, trying to replace what was gone, and locomotives were in particular demand. Dirks' production control at Skoda was helping in this area, while his lab helped in the other. It is interesting to note that both his work in data access and communications and his work in production control were keeping him out of the military service. He could have had two deferments, when deferments were very hard to come by. But deferment was only one of three incentives that drove him. He was working as hard as he could work.

The second incentive was a genuine concern for the German soldiers trapped in Russia. He would do what he could to find out what they needed and get it to them.

His third motivation was just beginning to take shape in the back of his mind. Supposing Germany lost the war? The possibility was looming. How could he make a living and support his family in a collapsed economy? A possible answer to that problem was what he was already working on for Germany. His ability to handle data would be of interest to corporations within the Western nations—not only in connection with communications, but also in connection with data going in and out of machines. He had the foresight to know that the computer industry was due for rapid growth. He was working on ideas and concepts that would be part of that growth.

Assuming Germany lost the war, how could he protect his inventions? Where could he hide his design work and where could he put the invaluable parts? How could he protect his ideas until they could be patented?

The more he pondered the problem the more he realized that there simply was no sure-fire solution. In all probability he would be facing a time of economic and social chaos. There would be no place anywhere that would be available to him, no place that would positively remain safe, in all of Germany. Finally he decided on Bad Langensalza. It was quite far west, it was not a strategic military or economic center, so it might survive the war intact. He would put his things there, and from there, when the time was right, he should be able to move them to where he would need them.

Consequently, when the three of them boarded the train Saturday morning, west-bound for Langensalza, Gerhard had distributed things neatly. In his wife's clothing and in his son's clothing, he had hidden preliminary drawings of electronic devices he was developing. In the food basket, which he carried, he had buried the small discreet parts that, after the war, might be irreplaceable.

The risk involved in carrying such things was comparatively slight. His credentials were exemplary. His trip was under the protective permission of the S.S. His papers from Skoda were in order. He had little to worry about until he returned to Prague alone, having used only one of the return passes.

As soon as he arrived in Langensalza and saw his family united with their maternal relatives, he took his leave and caught the next train back to Prague to face the music. The authorities would be furious. He didn't mind because he had most of his family well west of the Elbe River, where, he believed, they would be in the American Sector. He had saved them from the Russians.

He was wrong. Due to the senseless generosity of the American government at Potsdam, where the previous agreement at Yalta was further confirmed, the dictator Stalin was to be handed Eastern Europe and much of Germany. His family was soon to be in terrible danger. It was going to be harder to get them west from Bad Langensalza than it would have been from Prague.

* * *

Back at Skoda in Prague, Dirks' director was furious. The two men were in the director's office, Dirks standing at attention in front of the huge desk and the director sitting behind it reading. There was a third man in the room, the chief personnel officer, a major in the S.S. He had the mark on his collar that signified the branch of the S.S.

that was not clerical. He was the real thing. Gerhard correctly guessed that what was being read by the director was the file on Dirks that had been brought in by the Major. The officer was standing at the edge of the room looking out the window at the street below.

The file contained an impressive story. It started with Voss, the president of the largest accounting firm in Germany. He had been asked by Goering's organization to put together a committee of executives to examine the methods of accounting and production control used by all major German industrial firms. The best ideas thus gleaned were to be spread among the smaller German firms that lacked the manpower and know-how needed to attain maximum production goals.

Dr. Voss turned the matter of forming and directing the committee over to his friends and associates. Among those who were involved directly and indirectly were Dr. Kinne and Dr. Petzold, two influential men who became acquainted with Gerhard Dirks. Their power and influence were important to Gerhard later in his life.

When the committee was formed Gerhard Dirks was on it. His position with Mercedes Bueromischine-Gmbh had given him useful insight into the inner workings of big corporations and it was natural that he was chosen. The committee members, including Gerhard, were sent on information-gathering trips to all the major German businesses. In due time the book was written, it became a Bible of German business procedures, and the information was efficiently dispersed.

The file showed that when the Berlin headquarters had been bombed into rubble, Dirks, who had distinguished himself as a member of the committee, had been sent to Prague to implement those things that he had learned and described in his reports, the best in modern production and accounting procedures.

The director finished the dossier and looked up at Gerhard. "I'm surprised that a man who has served the Fatherland so well, and who has in the past shown himself trustworthy would stoop to a trick."

There didn't seem to be a good answer to that, so Gerhard held his silence. The director spoke again.

"There are many of us, Herr Dirks, who would like to send our families to a safer place, but we believe in the victory of Germany and our faith in the Fuhrer is intact."

That was a lie and Gerhard knew it. The director just hadn't been able to think of a way to get his family north or west. "Let me assure you, Herr Direktor . . . "

The S.S. officer spoke for the first time, addressing Dirks. "Shut up."

Gerhard maintained an immediate and complete silence. His director spoke again. "You are no longer the controller. You will keep your production program going with your cards. You will exercise no other authority and you will take no other responsibilities. All executive privileges are here and now rescinded. Now go back to work."

The S.S. man spoke again. "Just a moment, Dirks." It was a rude way to address a man in Gerhard's position. "There will be no more travel permits granted to you or to anyone related to you. Do not even attempt to apply."

Gerhard snapped his heels, said "Heil" and left the room, breathing a little easier. His feeling had been confirmed, they needed him to run the production control. Nothing else would have persuaded the S.S. officer to let him live. He had felt the hate.

It was a good bargain. Step two was completed, most of his family was west of the Elbe, and he'd lost only his executive privileges and his right to travel. The first bothered him not at all, the second could be a problem. He'd have to think of a way around that prohibition. He thought of a way when he was thinking about how he would make a living for his family in Bad Langensalza.

That night, from his lab in Roztoky he called Huth, the commercial manager of the Power's Subsidiary in Berlin. Would Huth send a truck to the lab in Roztoky and have it pick up the lab equipment? Gerhard wanted it moved to Sommerda. Huth said he would do it. There was no direct connection between his Berlin office and the Sommerda facility, but there were people over him who could arrange it, and he would see that it was done. Also, would Huth arrange for a travel permit to go from Prague to Berlin? Gerhard wanted to talk to

Dr. Petzold about a data access development. Huth agreed to arrange for it.

Talking to Dr. Petzold about data access development wasn't the whole story. He wanted to talk to Dr. Petzold about a job at the facility at Sommerda and have Dr. Petzold transfer him there.

Sommerda had several advantages. It was well west of the Elbe River and would be in the American sector. It was close to Bad Langensalza. He would be able to go to Sommerda officially and then slip down to see his family. At Sommerda, with the equipment from Roztoky at his disposal, he should be able to develop something quickly that would interest the American manufacturers of office machines. He had already made the contacts he would need to gain their interest in him. So far, so good.

* * *

As the German military situation in the East deteriorated rapidly, Gerhard made his plans to leave Prague. He contacted Huth at the Berlin office and told him to issue the pass for Herr Doktor Gerhard Dirks to go from Prague to Berlin. (Once there, he was sure Dr. Petzold would give him a transfer to Sommerda.) During the first week in April of 1945 the pass came. It was issued to him as director of the lab, and because of the nature of Gerhard's experiments, Huth had had no problem getting the Berlin S.S. to approve Dr. Dirks' travel. The S.S. in Berlin didn't know what the S.S. in

Prague was thinking. Communications within the force were breaking down. The pass for Gerhard's mother, the only relative still living in the Prague area, came automatically. By the first week in April the ultimate loss of Prague to the Russians was easily predictable. The S.S. issued orders to the effect that any German over sixty-five years of age could leave Prague at any time.

On Saturday, April 7th, Gerhard and his mother got on the train in downtown Prague and left for Berlin. Frau Dirks had an identification card showing her age, and Gerhard had a permit to travel from the Berlin S.S. As the train headed north and crossed the river, he looked out the window at Prague for what he believed would be his last look. He never expected to see it again and he was sure that after the Russian arrival it would never be the same.

Dirks had picked the right day to leave. Monday the ninth of April, the S.S. in Prague issued orders that all German executives in Skoda would be issued S.S. uniforms, and would wear them. There would be no more civilian German executives.

This not only prevented escape, it also meant that when the Russians arrived, the German executives were easily picked out. The lucky ones were shot on sight and their bodies thrown into piles to be bulldozed into open pits. Some of the less fortunate were crucified, nailed up and left to hang and die. The Czechs lost their smugness. They divided themselves into two classes. There were the

Communist Czechs who helped the Russians, some of whom had scores to settle and were the most sadistic of all. Then there was the other Czechs who thought that the end of German domination would mean freedom. For them the light began to dawn. They were exchanging the Nazi frying pan for the Communist fire.

The Nazi invasion of Czechoslovakia brought terror to the anti-Nazi and the Jew. Except for the Czech Communists, the Russian invasion brought deprivation and terror to all. The Germans had sown a wind. The Russian whirlwind flew a red flag.

* * *

The train worked its way north and west to Berlin through Dresden. Dresden's destruction was complete but never completely explained. It was not a military target of note. There was little war-related industry. Its crime was to shelter refugees who were fleeing west from the Russian advance. The bombs and the subsequent fire had destroyed everything that could be seen from the railroad tracks. What could not be seen were the estimated 100,000 women and children who were burned or had suffocated when the fire used all the oxygen.

North of Dresden the terrain leveled out, and the hilly green belt of Southern Germany gave way to the northern flat lands. Square miles of Germany looked as they had looked for centuries, and the sight did not prepare the observer for the sudden appearance of a destroyed and desolate town with its damaged railway yard through which the train crept slowly, rocking its way over the uneven road bed. Gerhard steeled himself for Berlin. It had been bad when he left, he knew it would be worse when he got back, but he had not envisioned the destruction. It would be difficult to do so without seeing the physical evidence first hand. He turned his eyes away from the window and looked at his mother who was sitting across from him. She was looking out the window and quietly weeping.

"This is so stupid." Gerhard spoke with bitterness. "We could have been the leading industrial power in this whole part of the world."

She shook her head. "You don't understand. Never mind the buildings, they can be put up again; think of the suffering. I have no doubt that London looks like this too, and it was first to go."

"He should never have gone to war, it was not necessary."

"It was not him," his mother replied, "It is Satan. No human could think this into existence."

Gerhard had his own ideas on that subject. To him, Satan was a mythical figure from his childhood days. In his own mind he was a solidly convinced atheist, but his parents were Lutheran and he had been educated, confirmed and baptized into the German Lutheran Church. Those beliefs had been long abandoned, but this was not the time to tell his mother.

"Maybe so, Mama, maybe so." He spoke more gently. "I will also believe in miracles if the apartment building with my apartment in it is still standing."

It was, though this failed to lead him to believe in miracles. There were several blocks of buildings that had sustained no damage. In the center of this, his apartment building and his apartment stood intact. Gerhard and his mother had left the ruined train station and, on foot, picked their way through piles of rubble to where the buildings still stood in the Nikolassee section.

They made their way up the stairs to the second floor. Frau Dirks' left knee had healed well, and her right one was better, but it still troubled her, especially climbing stairs. Gerhard had a key to his apartment, but it was subleased to a Mrs. Schneider so he knocked and waited.

When she came to the door Gerhard was slightly repulsed by her seedy appearance. Then he remembered that his clothes were not in the best condition either. In April of 1945, there were few people in Berlin who were neatly dressed.

Mrs. Schneider did not recognize them, and stood waiting for them to speak. Her tired face was set in lines that showed she was ready to say "no" to whatever was asked. Behind her Gerhard could see several children sitting on the floor playing. That would be the total of the apartment's occupants, women and children. There would be no men. He could understand her hardness. Here was a man at the door in civilian clothes, what was he— Gestapo? He spoke in a conciliatory manner.

"I'm Gerhard Dirks and this is my mother."

Her face softened. "I did not recognize you; come in."

Permission to enter had been given, but not the traditional, cheerful German welcome. She was frightened and nervous.

"What brings you to Berlin?"

"I want to see some people who are connected with my business."

"You work for Skoda, don't you?" She hadn't suggested that they sit down.

"Yes."

"They sent you to Berlin?"

"No, Skoda didn't send me." Then Gerhard realized what was troubling her. She didn't want the S.S. to walk in and find her harboring a fugitive or a deserter. "I have papers."

He produced the S.S. authority for his trip to Berlin and Mrs. Schneider looked relieved. "You and your mother will want to stay here?"

"Just for a night or two. We're sorry to inconvenience you, but there is no place else." They were standing in the center of the living room. Gerhard remembered the pleasant days spent in the apartment with his family, and then later, the horrible nights when the bombs were falling. Mrs. Schneider had not changed the apartment in any way, nor altered the furnishings, now shabby with age and use, but the war shortages had made one unpleasant change. The apartment was cold. The early spring sun had not heated the building and there was no other source of warmth.

"Do you have food stamps?" It was obvious she had no desire to share what little food she had.

"For Prague only." He pointed to the basket he had carried from the train. "We have a little food left."

"Good, and with your papers, you can register for stamps. Do you know where to go?"

"Yes. We passed the place on the way here. I will get them and I will see if the people I want to talk to are still in Berlin. My mother will wait for me here." He paused for a moment before he asked the next question and then decided it would hurt nothing to ask. "There used to be a man named Kostka who rented the little house we had rented before we bought this apartment. By any chance, has he come here looking for us? We were friends."

She thought a moment. "There was a man who came by that name. If I remember him correctly, he said he was going into the military, the army, I think." She looked at Dirks carefully. "You are a brave man to go out on the street in civilian clothes."

"It is not always pleasant," Gerhard admitted, "but I carry my papers in my hand. That way I don't get stopped as often."

She nodded her understanding and Gerhard took his leave.

SAN FRANCISCO, CALIFORNIA, 32 years later. Gerhard Dirks gazes out the window of his hillside home. He says it doesn't hurt to recall the long-past traumas of his early life.

"Remembering is sometimes helpful," he comments in a heavy German accent. "Maybe we won't do again what we once did before. Also, by looking back, one can see cycles in one's own life and in cultures. Maybe something I say will help someone else.

"Sometimes we do learn from history. I believe that history is repeating itself. But let me tell you something about looking back. You look back and remember things that you did and regret doing. That is bad, but not as bad as something else. The worst is what you didn't do and regret not doing—that is what hurts. You don't realize at the time how important it is."

He leans forward in his chair, punching out with his index finger to emphasize what he is saying.

"Such things are most important, for by doing nothing, the day comes when you share in the guilt of those who did actively wrong. You share not just in the blame, you share in the guilt, too, but that you do not see at the time.

"One day, early in Hitler's rise to power, my associate and I were on our way back to the factory from lunch and we heard some glass breaking. We were a little early, due not yet back at the office, so we went to see why glass was breaking. It was the windows of a Jewish store. There were some S.S. there with clubs. They were breaking and destroying and laughing.

"*My friend and I stood with twenty or thirty other Germans across the street from them and watched. We said to each other, 'Should we do something?' If any of us had moved, I think the others would have helped. We did nothing. Why? Fear, and fear becomes a way of life. I will tell some more stories about fear and how it is instilled and how it grows.*

"*The second time such a thing happened was on a streetcar. The law had just been passed that all Jews had to wear the star of David. A woman got on the car and there were no seats so she stood in the aisle. When I was young, that was not done, that a man should sit and a woman stand. A gentleman gave his seat to a lady. I looked down at the young Nazi sitting in front of me to say something like, 'How can you not give up your seat?' Then I saw it. She had on the star of David. I believe to this day that if I had spoken, the German men on the car would have helped me stand him on his feet, but I said nothing. The day came very soon when such things did not bother me at all any more. The organized and dedicated minority, in the end, dominates the inept majority. You find yourself going along. Then you, too, are guilty. You will always wonder, 'Had I spoken, had I acted, would things have been different?' It will always haunt you.*"

He is silent for a moment.

"*The problem is like a programmed computer. A man programs himself by his deep desires—maybe he's not even aware of some of them—by his environment, and by the sum total of all previous decisions.*

It is true, there can be more—but in those days I didn't know that. So, we see most people like machines putting together an answer to a question and the answer is the product of what has gone before and has been stored, consciously and subconsciously.

"This is why it is so important in our culture here in America today, to see what goes into our young people, from their entertainment, from their education. Is there much that makes for what you might call 'standing power'? The input that makes possible a real choice? I don't think so. The things that happened in pre-Nazi Germany are beginning to happen here in this country.

"First, there is a question about how can something be right and something else be wrong? We are told that moral absolutes are all nonsense. White becomes grey and black becomes grey. You cannot expect a computer to come up with the correct answer if you have excluded from the input necessary information. You cannot expect a young person to stand openly for what is right when everything that gives him input, all his culture, its entertainment, its news and its educational system, are based on a theory of relative values. The information needed to make one stand up against social pressures, the reason for standing, is being programmed out of the young human machine in America.

"It is not good."

THREE

The office building that had housed the Power's organization had been damaged and the company had moved across the hall to smaller quarters, but quarters that were still usable. Dirks walked in and spoke to the secretary at the reception desk.

"I am Gerhard Dirks."

She nodded. "I have been expecting you. Both Herr Huth and Herr Becker spoke of you."

Huth was the business manager of the Power's office and Becker was the technical man. They had worked well together for years.

"They are not here?"

"No."

"When will they be back?"

"They will not be back."

"Can you tell me where they went?"

"To Frankfurt."

That would be well within the American zone. "Can you tell me how they got transferred?"

"Huth just re-assigned himself, and Herr Becker too."

The girl didn't look at him, she looked at the typewriter on her desk. Because she was at the office, she looked business-like, but underneath that she was very pretty, Dirks noticed.

"Where can I find Dr. Petzel or Dr. Roener?" Roener was Petzel's boss, and either man could help him.

"They are gone too."

"Did they happen to leave anything for me?"

"No. They mentioned you, but they left nothing. What do you need?" When Gerhard didn't answer she guessed. "A transfer someplace?"

"It would have been helpful."

"I'll type one and sign Dr. Petzel's name to it for you."

That would be fine now, but it might come back to haunt him. He'd just make it to Sommerda on brass and grit. He looked at the girl again.

"Fraulein, why don't you type a transfer for yourself? Why stay in Berlin?"

"A pass or a transfer would do me no good. I live in a hole in a wall with my mother and my little son. They are both sick and the one is too old and the other too young to travel. I cannot leave them."

"Your husband?"

"He's dead."

There were tears in her eyes now, and Gerhard spoke quietly. "I understand and I'm sorry."

He turned and left the office, leaving the girl there alone, consigned to a fate known only to God.

* * *

The next day, Gerhard and his mother walked to the train station to look the situation over. The place was mobbed. In the past, no matter how badly the station had been bombed the night before, the next day a sense of orderliness was restored. Now that was gone. No one cared any more. Gerhard knew that as far as getting on the train was concerned he didn't need any authority sending him to Sommerda. In the state of complete confusion that now reigned in the train station, nobody was looking at anyone's authority to go anywhere.

There was a make-shift wire gate covering the passageway to a waiting train. A sign, hand written, had been hung on the wire, MAGDEBURG. That city was in the general direction that Gerhard wanted to travel. A quick look around the station showed other trains going south and southeast, but this seemed to be the only one westward bound.

He turned to his mother. "Mama, how's your knee?"

"Tired, but still working."

"I'm going to try to get on that train." He pointed to the fourth car from the rear. "I shall run for that car, the fourth from here. I will try to get a seat. You come as quickly as you can. I'll try to save two seats, but I'll get at least one for you. I can run faster if I don't have the suitcases, can you carry them both that far?"

"Yes." She was numb in mind, body and spirit. She had only begun to adjust to the death of her husband, and now she was watching the death of her country. Gerhard was her one link with reality. She would do whatever he asked.

They stood and waited for hours. When the "gate" was opened there was a surge of humanity. Gerhard ran unencumbered. Being one of the first on the car, he grabbed a seat facing forward and sat sideways to hold two places.

It didn't work. By the time his mother arrived, the car was so jammed that no seat could be saved and people were standing in the aisle. He had been pushed to one inside seat. When she got there with their bags, he put the suitcases on the floor and sat on them and put his mother in the seat.

The train sat for an hour before it moved. When it did, the steam from the engine came through the pipes to the passenger car and took the chill of the evening away. It felt good at first, and then, as the car warmed, the smell of unwashed human bodies packed in together became an overwhelming stench. The train proceded slowly, rocking from side to side. They crept through the heavily bombed railroad yards of Potsdam and then entered more open country. The clouds that had been forming all day gradually lowered and began to drop their rain. It was a blessing. The Allied fighter plane attacks on trains were growing more infrequent anyway, but with the low clouds and rain, there wouldn't be any at all. Light could be turned on, inside and out.

Around ten thirty that night, the train slowed down gradually. Finally it stopped. Leaving his suitcase in the aisle near Frau Dirks, Gerhard decided to try to find out why they weren't moving. He'd had about all of the inside of the car that he could stand anyway. Outside, he found that the rain had diminished to something that was somewhere between a slight drizzle and a heavy fog. He stood by the passenger car letting his eyes adjust. In a few moments he could see well enough to walk forward toward the engine. The light coming through the passenger car windows lit his way.

There were twelve cars before he got to the engine. It stood on the tracks, a stationary but breathing thing, its parts giving an occasional clank in response to steam pressure. There was a group of men standing in the middle of the tracks ahead of the engine, lit up by the head light. Gerhard joined them. He had been giving orders to the people around him for years and his voice had taken on a note of authority. People were inclined to do what he said, or answer what he asked, and then think about it later.

"You are the conductor?"

"Yes, Mein Herr."

"I'm Doktor Dirks." He said it as though the conductor should know that that name meant something. The conductor was not about to say that he didn't know who Dr. Dirks was. "What is our problem?"

"Herr Doktor, the bridge across the Elbe is gone. We were told that it was here yesterday. It is gone now. This is as far as we can go. We're discussing what to do. There does not seem much choice except to go back to Berlin."

Gerhard decided to stick his neck out, a little. What he was about to imply could be construed as treason. It was based on the admission that Germany had lost the war. He knew Germany had, and he thought it probable that the engineer, fireman, brakeman and conductor who formed the center of the little group were of the same opinion. People who tried to keep trains running had had their fill of the war. Still, one never knew when a fanatic was present, one who would scream or shoot at anyone who suggested that the war was lost. He would be careful.

"Could we not sit here until daylight and then see if there is some other way across the river?"

"No, Herr Doktor. We believe that the Americans are on the other side of the river. In the morning, they will be able to see the train and we are within artillery range. Then there are rumors, Herr Dokter."

"What rumors?"

"The Americans have made an agreement with the Russians. If you try to cross the river, the Americans will shoot you. If you get across and are found without local papers, they will turn you over to the Russians."

Gerhard exploded. "It could not be true."

The rest of the group maintained a discreet silence. They knew the truth had been spoken, but they didn't want to argue with him.

At the moment, to Dirks, what the Americans

were or were not doing was not a pressing matter. He could not swim across the cold, swollen Elbe by himself, much less get across with his mother. Any boat available would be priced out of sight. His money was limited and he didn't want to spend it like that. Also, the story about the Americans shooting could be true. He had heard the Czech nationals discussing American policy back at the Skoda plant. In the opinion of the Czechs, the Americans were very naive and did not know that once Germany was gone, Russia would be her mortal enemy. Fortunately, he had put his family west of the Elbe weeks before. They were with his wife's people and would have local papers and local acknowledgement. The problem at hand was how to join them.

He spoke again with authority. "Take us back to Berlin. But do not leave too soon."

The implication, unspoken, was that anyone who wanted to get off the train and try to get across to the American side should be given a chance to do so.

Dirks had made the decision that they would have all liked to make but had been a little fearful. Now someone who had authority, or seemed to have authority had made the decision for them. The conductor was grateful.

"Thank you, Herr Dokter."

They started back to the train as a group and then each climbed aboard where he belonged. The engineer and the firemen entered the engine cab.

The conductor would signal them to start backing after he had made his announcement to the last group of passengers in the last car. The conductor climbed aboard the first car and made his first announcement.

"The bridge over the Elbe is out. The Americans are on the other side of the river and have blown it up. We will take this train back to Berlin in a few minutes."

Gerhard and the other passengers who had formed the group returned to their respective cars. Gerhard found his mother sleeping. As he sat back down on the suitcases he looked at her. The healthy Hausfrau had disappeared. In her place there was a very tired old lady whose clothes now hung loosely on her shrunken frame. Her face had lost its fullness and looked genuinely gaunt. Gerhard set his jaw. He'd find a way to get her to the west.

When the conductor made his announcement in Gerhard's car, there was a minute or two of conversation and then several passengers left. They were middle-aged men traveling alone, and three middle-aged couples. When they left there was more room on the car. Gerhard lifted his bags to the racks over the seats and took an empty place behind his mother. The ride back to Berlin would be more comfortable. The train jerked and started backing. It backed all the way to Zerbst before there was switching available to turn it around. He looked at his watch. It was after midnight. That made it the tenth of April. He didn't know how many days he'd have before the Russians would be in Berlin, but he knew he didn't have many. And it would be the Russians. If it were to be the Americans, they would have left the bridge over the river intact and they would have been using it. They must have agreed to let the Russians in either first, or at the same time. Either way, it was bad.

* * *

The depot had not changed in twenty-four hours. It was still mobbed. Gerhard looked at the various tracks. There were no more trains westbound. That meant that the rumors about the Americans were probably true. They had not only reached the Elbe, they were holding it for the Russians and they would shoot any German who was trying to get away. He was forced to believe the rumors because of the lack of westbound trains. It would be logical in the state of affairs present that all the trains would be headed west toward the Americans. There was none.

If he could not go west, he could go south and then west. If he reached the green belt of Germany he could walk. It was hard to track someone down in that part of Europe. They'd take the train back toward Chemitz, and get off before they got there.

The southbound train was as jammed as the westbound had been; people tried anything to get out of Berlin. Once again his mother took an aisle seat and he sat on their luggage. The "gate" had been marked Chemitz and Gerhard had expected the train to take a different route out of town, but it used the same tracks that the train had used the day before. He guessed that any train leaving Berlin would be confined to one or two routes that were kept in a state of semi-repair. All other routes would be left in their wrecked condition. There wasn't enough material and labor to keep everything in working order. The train turned south and took a single track route to Luckenwalds. There it joined the main line that was headed toward Wittenberg, but at Juterburg it turned south again and was on the single track that went to Chemitz via Riesa. The track had suffered little war damage, so the train picked up speed and made time as it would have before the war. It was still daylight when they stopped at the town of Waldheim.

That was as far in that direction that the train would go. The conductor was told that there were Americans coming north and if the train continued on its journey it would run into them. The rumors were not yet true, and later trains continued on their way south, but the conductor had no way of knowing true from false and so used prudence. He decided to take his train back to Riesa and then use the track to Dresden and from there, they would try to go south again. That would not help Gerhard. He would not be going far enough south to make up for the extra distance east. He decided to get off in Waldheim.

For some reason the name of the town was

sticking in his mind. Suddenly it came to him. He had had a sweetheart back at the University, a girl named Vera, who had been on her way to becoming a pediatrician. He had been on his way to his doctorate of laws. She had moved to Waldheim and opened a practice. He had received a letter from her after her move, and then she had married and he had heard no more.

What was her married name?

Gerhard approached the station master. Yes, it was a good day, yes it might rain tomorrow, one could feel it in the air. Did the station master know a doctor, a pediatrician, her first name, Vera? Of course the station master did, she was a well-thought-of doctor and well known in the area. She had married a young man named Schmidt and practiced under that name.

Gerhard proffered a bill. "You have change for the telephone?" He pointed to it on the station wall.

The station master refused the bill. "No one comes for the coins anymore. One of our electricians re-wired it around the coin box. Call anywhere you like. If the line is still working you will get an answer."

Gerhard thanked him, walked over to the phone and looked for the number in the battered phone book. He fixed her address in his mind and then memorized the number before he called it.

Vera answered. "Dr. Schmidt speaking."

"This is Doktor Dirks."

"Gerhard, where are you?" There was genuine

warmth in her voice.

"Here in Waldheim." Conversation can be difficult when an intimate relationship that was dropped is re-opened. What does one ask? He decided on the mundane. "How are things with you?"

"Fine, thank you. I have a baby girl, and I'm still practicing medicine as much as I can. Medicines are hard to come by."

The awkward question. "Where is your husband?"

"I have received the official announcement that he is dead."

Gerhard thought to himself that he should have known that. Everyone's husband was dead. "I'm sorry to hear that."

"You are alone?" She would want to know if he was married.

"No. I have my mother. The rest of my family is west of the Elbe." There was no need to say Bad Langensalza over the phone.

"The Elbe will not do. The Americans stopped at the Mulde."

"They are west of the Mulde."

There was a moment's silence while she made up her mind to take the risk. "You'll want a place to stay and it is better if you are not seen. Any man of military age in or out of uniform is under suspicion. So, do not come to the office. I will give you my residence address. You have something to write on?"

"I don't need to write."

She laughed, "I remember now, you remember everything." She gave him her address. "For the moment, go to the Inn of the Hungry Lion, it is a mile in back of the train station. They are good people who own it. Stay there until dark and then leave by the back door. Walk to my house and come to my back door. Try not to be seen."

Gerhard was grateful. "Thank you."

"Not at all, it will be like old times to see you again." She hung up.

Gerhard turned to his mother. "Come, Mama, we shall soon be with friends. I will get you something to eat."

* * *

Gerhard knocked on the kitchen door at the back of Vera's house. The light in the kitchen went out.

"Who's there?"

"Gerhard."

The door opened and Gerhard and his mother walked in.

"We won't turn on the light down here. Follow me upstairs. There is less chance of being seen."

The second floor bedroom was nicely furnished. There was not only a large bed and a crib with a sleeping baby, there were two large, comfortable chairs. Vera helped Frau Dirks take her coat off; the upstairs part of the house was comfortably warm.

Gerhard looked at Vera. She was thinner than she had been during her medical school days, but who in Germany wasn't thinner in these times? It made her high cheek bones seem even higher and the blue eyes were deeper in her face and, if anything, bluer. It brought back pleasant memories.

"Why so much secrecy?" Gerhard asked.

"The bugs are coming out from under the rocks."

"What do you mean?"

"There are a few Communists in town who will be entering their glory. Suddenly they have many friends. You were a Party Member, no?"

"Yes, but who wasn't?"

"Many now claim they weren't. Where is your family?"

Gerhard had seated himself in the other chair and Vera sat on her bed. "In Bad Langensalza."

"Good, you should be all right if you can get there."

"Why shouldn't I get there?"

"Where are you supposed to be now?"

"Prague."

"So, the S.S. would like to talk to you. The Communists have something special for you if they find and identify you. There are two kinds of Communists, German and Russian, and the Americans will be looking for you. They will be the hardest to stay away from."

"Why? What are they doing?"

"First, they are on the other side of the Mulde River. They are holding Germans back for the attacking Russians. If you try to cross the bridge, they will shoot you. If you try to get across the river any other way and they see you, they will shoot you. If you get across and are walking west, they will put you in a stockade and ship you back to the Russians. Then you will wish they had shot you."

Frau Dirks had begun to snore.

"Your mother is exhausted."

"Yes, but she will be more exhausted before we see Langensalza." He changed the subject. "How has your practice been, Doktor?" Gerhard asked it with a gracious smile.

"Too good. The men doctors have gone with the army. The only other doctor in Waldheim is seventy-five years old. I'm not a pediatrician any more—I do everything. The people in the town are afraid I will leave, that is why I have heat for the house, and potatoes." That reminded her. "You and your mother are hungry, Gerhard?"

"Yes. They wouldn't sell us anything to eat at the Inn."

"I will go downstairs and get a couple of baked potatoes. Just a minute."

When she left the room Gerhard got up out of his chair and walked over to the crib and looked at the sleeping baby. He was sure it was more than three or four months old, maybe six months. That would mean that Vera had seen her husband over a year ago. He wondered if she had seen him since, probably not. Germany was full of babies who had never seen their fathers, and many never would.

Vera returned with a cold, baked potato in each hand. She woke Frau Dirks and gave her one and

Gerhard the other. Frau Dirks was starving, she wolfed the potato down and then went back to sleep.

"She is too tired to go to bed." Gerhard had eaten his potato as fast as his mother had eaten hers. "Do you have a blanket we could put over her and let her sleep there?"

"Certainly." Vera took the quilt off the foot of her bed and wrapped it around the old lady.

"You have another room down the hall for me?" Gerhard asked.

Vera just looked at him silently. He got the message, and was pleased.

FOUR

For the next two days, Gerhard watched the German Army retreat. It wasn't really a retreat, it was a rout. The Army that had been the terror of Europe walked by, disheveled, dispirited and defeated. They retreated to Waldheim where they got the word that the Americans were at the Mudle. So, they turned north up the road that ran to the center of Germany. Many walked down the road that ran in front of Vera's house. Gerhard stood back from the second floor window and looked out at them. It was a sad sight, and it would be followed by a worse one. The Russians were coming. Some of the men in Waldheim had started to build a barricade at the east end of town, something to help them put up a little resistance. The retreating Germans had talked them out of it.

One of the soldiers had been specific. "Don't get the Russians angry. They'll blow your city off the face of the earth."

The third night, when Vera returned from her office she had bad news. "Someone has seen you and knows you are here. There are questions now. Why are you hiding? Are you a deserter? Are you a high Nazi? Also, the Russians are supposed to be here in three days, four at the most. We must do something."

Gerhard had a plan. He had been memorizing the maps of south central Germany that Vera had loaned him and he was ready to start his trip. He did not think it wise to let the two women in on the details; it might make it hard for them to answer questions they might be asked, and answer in a natural way. He planned to go to the local military and tell them that he wanted a pass back to Prague where he belonged. Anyone could get a pass to Prague, few questions asked. Once on the train and headed in that direction he would get off as soon as possible and walk back to Waldheim under cover of darkness. Then he, his mother, and the baby and Vera, if she wanted to go, would leave during the darkness and start walking west. Vera had triggered the plan when she had told Gerhard that she knew a man in Colditz who rowed people across the river, for a price.

Gerhard broke the silence. "I had better go back to Prague where I belong."

His mother was adamant. "No, never. They will kill you."

"They will kill me here just as quickly, and if you are with me they will kill you, too."

There were tears, there were arguments, there was cajoling, all to no avail. Gerhard had made up his mind.

The next day Gerhard got his pass to Prague,

got on the train headed for Freiburg and got off the first time it stopped. After the train pulled out, he stayed near the station for a while to see if anyone was interested in him. If they were, they hid it well, and he started walking back to Waldheim. The overcast thickened and it began to rain—gently at first and then moderately. Finally it poured. By the time he reached Vera's kitchen door, he was drenched, cold and hungry. He knocked. There was no response. He couldn't make too much noise, the neighbors would hear him and the purpose of his trip would be frustrated.

In the darkness and the rain, he ran his hands over the wet ground near the house, until he had a dozen small stones. With these in hand he went around to the side of the house and began to throw the stones against Vera's bedroom window. A light came on and he ran around to the kitchen door and knocked again. This time there was a response. In a few moments Vera called from inside the kitchen.

"Who's there."

"Gerhard."

The door was opened immediately. "Come upstairs quickly."

When his mother saw him, she wept for joy. "Why did you not say you were coming back?" She wiped her eyes. "Do you not trust us?"

"I trust you, Mama, but you are not a very convincing liar. If someone said, 'Where is your son?' I wanted you to be able to say, 'He went to Prague' in such a way that they would believe you."

Later, dressed in dry clothes, Gerhard sat in the

large chair in the upstairs bedroom and gradually got warm. As he warmed up, he quit shaking. He looked at the young woman doctor; he was very fond of her.

"Vera, will you not come with us? Come as far as Sommerda. You are a doctor, you can practice anywhere. Why wait for the Russians? You know what might happen to you."

"I cannot walk across Southern Germany carrying my baby."

"We will help."

"Thank you, but I could not take her out in this rain, it would kill her. It will kill your mother too."

"We will wait until tomorrow night."

"What will I do with my baby if it rains next week?"

"We will be in the American sector then, some Germans will give us shelter."

"Maybe."

"There's something troubling you, Vera."

"Yes. There are men who are supposed to be alive but they are dead. There are men reported dead who are still alive. If my husband is alive— and I've never talked to anyone who saw his body, I have only the official report—he will come here, if he can. If I am not here, how will he find me?"

Gerhard had no answer and sat in silence. In a moment she continued. "I think I have the best chance of keeping my baby alive by staying here. The Russians will probably want a resident doctor, and this gives me a good chance of being allowed to live here. Also, if years from now my husband should come back like one from the dead, I will still be in Waldheim." The bedroom windows rattled slightly. "What was that?"

"Artillery," Gerhard answered grimly. "We leave tomorrow night, rain or no rain."

"I can send word to the man with the boat and make arrangements for you. When you leave here, walk to the edge of Colditz and circle the town to the river on the north side. Go north along the bank for about three kilometers. There will be a very small farm house with the stable attached to the back of it and a high picket fence around the yard in back of the stable. Knock on the front door four times and then wait. He has a row boat and he will row you across the Mulde. Have something with you to pay him." She looked at her watch. "It is after midnight. I will tell him that you will be at his house before dawn tomorrow."

"Thank you."

"You'll want to take the maps you were studying."

"No, if I have any maps on me, it is a giveaway. I'm a stranger." He tapped his head. "They are in here, all of them."

She smiled. It was the last time he ever saw her smile.

* * *

The Russian Army moved just as fast in the rain as it did in the sunshine. The morning saw them in Waldheim. There was a quiet about the city that was unnatural and the stream of German soldiers that had been filing past the house had ceased.

It was Anna Dirks who came up with the suggestion. Gerhard's mother did not lack courage. For a few days she had been comfortable and had had enough food to keep body and soul together. She was coming out of her lethargy.

"I am an old woman. The soldiers will not bother me. Let me go downtown and look around. Vera is too young and you are a man of military age. It is safe only for me."

"It's not safe for you either, Mama. I don't like it."

"It is better for us to know what is going on than to sit here and wonder." She got out of her chair and went to the hall closet for her coat.

Gerhard watched her go. He had a cold feeling in his stomach. They had waited in Waldheim one day too long. "Be careful Mama."

She said nothing and left. It was three hours before she returned. Gerhard knew by looking at her when she came in the room that things were not good. There was fear in her eyes.

"It is bad, Mama?"

She was taking off her coat. "It is terrible." She looked at Vera, "The office buildings are a shambles. Two Russian soldiers were there looking for valuables. They make a mess of anything they find locked. They just smash, smash, smash."

"Did they hurt you?"

"Not much. I made the mistake of having on

my rings. They tried to take them off me and I struggled yelling, 'My husband is dead, my husband is dead.' Finally they threw me down and left me my rings. When they were gone I took them off and put them in my pocket. Then I wandered around the city. There are Russians everywhere helping themselves to whatever they want. They go in twos and are heavily armed. I didn't see a single Russian who looked like an officer, they are all enlisted men. Also, there are no Germans in uniform anywhere. Everyone is in civilian clothes. I haven't seen a German city with no German uniforms for a long, long time." She turned to Vera, "There are terrible things going on in that city. You stay out of sight."

"I will if I can."

Gerhard heard something and moved to the window. There were two Russian soldiers pounding on the door of the house across from Vera's. When the door was not opened, one of the soldiers fired a couple of shots with his pistol and the door lock disintegrated. The soldiers walked in. In the street in front of the house, a horse drawn wagon stood, a wagon loaded with household furnishings and clothing, whatever had struck the Russian fancy as they raided the houses.

"Are your neighbors home?" Gerhard asked.

"They slipped out last night, I think."

"Why don't we go out the back as the soldiers come in the front?"

"No, Gerhard. I'm going to stay. If we go out the back, someone will see you and they will know you are back. Then after you are gone, they will ask me where you went and it will be trouble for me, and for you too if they catch you. Leave the door unlatched. When the Russians come in, they will not know you do not belong here. They will think you are my husband. Let them take what they want."

"They may want you."

"Maybe, but if what your mother says is true, they may be satiated. Maybe last night they had all they can handle. I think it is better to wait."

When the soldiers first came in, Vera's decision seemed the wise one. They were interested in things. A coat out of the closet was thrown on the floor to act as a carrying device. Bric-a-brack, more clothing, silverware and related items were thrown on the pile while the Germans watched. Vera wasn't too upset, she'd buried her more cherished possessions months before. One of the soldiers spoke to her.

She thought he said "cake." The Russian word for kitchen and the German word for cake sound alike. She went into the kitchen to get a small piece of cake she had made for her daughter's six-month birthday. She came back out of the kitchen with the small cake on a dish. Gerhard was worried; the men were disheveled and dissipated. Also, they were drunk but not drunk enough. They would not be easy to control.

With a stupid and uncomprehending countenance, the Russian soldier looked at the cake in Vera's hand for a moment. Then he let out a snarl.

He knocked the cake out of her hand and the plate broke against the wall. Yelling "Kitchen" in Russian again he shoved her toward it. He followed her.

Gerhard started after them, and the second soldier stuck a pistol into Gerhard's chest and said something in Russian. Gerhard stood still, looking at the smiling Russian.

Dirks kept looking at the Russian, trying to figure the meaning of the smile. Did the man want him to take the gun away, and go help Vera? The Russian nodded his head "yes" almost imperceptably. Anna Dirks kept her eyes riveted on the soldier and her son. Gerhard waited, not moving a muscle.

When the first soldier was through with Vera, he came back into the room. The man holding the pistol on Gerhard said something in Russian and smiled. His friend laughed. Then Gerhard watched the man in front of him slowly move his second hand from behind his back. It contained a pistol. He had hoped that Gerhard would reach for the first pistol and then be killed by the second one. Not moving had saved Gerhard's life for a few more minutes, but he knew the end was coming now. The Russian looked at him and began, Gerhard guessed, to call him filthy names in Russian. Anna Dirks knew what was going to happen and it was too much for her. She ran from her place against the wall straight at the Russian yelling in German, "No, shoot me, shoot me."

She knocked the guns away and got between the soldier and her son. The soldier looked at the old lady in silence for a moment, and then in a way that sentimental drunks will do, he began to cry and say "Mama, mama."

He put his pistols back in his belt and reached out with an empty hand and patted Frau Dirks on the head. His friend pushed him away from her and pointed to the loot still on the floor. He spoke in Russian and the soldier responded. They picked up the coat filled with Vera's things and made their way clumsily out the front door to their wagon.

Vera came into the room from the kitchen walking with obvious pain. Her clothes were torn and her mouth was bleeding where the Russian had hit her. "That hurt," she said softly.

Gerhard spoke to her quietly. "Vera, will you come with us now?"

"Why? What more can they do to me?"

"They can come back."

"Maybe, but there are too many other women."

"The Russian swine."

"From what I've heard, the Russians have a majority of the swine, but they do not have a monopoly. I'm a doctor and I have treated women who were abused by German soldiers. The Russian was drunk and having his problems and his friend wasn't interested. It was rough enough, but compared with what I've seen as a doctor, I got off lightly."

"And the next time?"

"Next time, I won't resist." She looked at Gerhard. "Help me upstairs. It hurts to walk."

Gerhard picked her up and carried her to the floor above. He turned his head away from the signs of abuse and left Vera with his mother. Back downstairs he sat and stared out the window. His mother had saved his life. He must save hers.

* * *

There was an early morning mist close to the river. Gerhard was within a few feet of it before he saw it. It was smooth and placid at that point and what was left of the moon shown through the light mist and in a fuzzy way, reflected itself on the surface. Gerhard motioned to his mother to follow and turned down stream. They walked quietly and cautiously. The back yards of some of the residences on the outskirts of town went all the way to the river's edge. Gerhard was a little worried when he heard a dog bark. He fervently hoped that the animal would not come to investigate.

Soon they were beyond the well-kept yards and were in farm country. They lost the sliver of moon and the darkness was almost total. Because of the darkness and the mist, Gerhard almost missed the place Vera had described. It wasn't as close to the river as he had expected. He made his way to the door and knocked four times. The silence that followed seemed endless. About the time he was sure he had the wrong house, the door opened. The man who opened it signaled for them to come in.

The small light coming from the kitchen seemed bright after the darkness of the early morning. Gerhard could see the man, large and surly with malcontent written on his face.

"You are too late. It will be light before I return; someone may see me. I won't go unless I'm well-paid."

Gerhard took off his coat and handed it to the man. It was a beautiful garment, and in the winter that was coming, under Russian occupation, it might save the wearer's life. It would be of little immediate use to Gerhard. Winter was passing and with it the cold. Next year would have to take care of itself.

The man took the coat into the kitchen and examined it. The coat had been expensive even by pre-disaster standards. Now, nothing like it could be found in Germany at any price. The fine materials were not available. He came back into the room.

"What else do you have?"

Gerhard had money sewn into his luggage and his clothing. He meant to use it when he rejoined his family, and he meant to be very careful with it, but he had expected to be asked for more than the coat and he had taken an amount which he considered reasonable and had it ready. When the man asked for more, Gerhard put his hand in his pocket and pulled out all the money in it.

"This will have to do, my friend, the coat and the cash."

There was a grunt, followed by, "This way."

They went out the back door, away from the river and used a path that, in a sweeping semicircle, led to the bank of the Mulde. At the water's edge there was a rowboat. It looked as slovenly as its owner, and had an inch or two of water in the bottom. Gerhard guessed that from time to time he just bailed it out rather than bother to fix it. The man shoved the boat into the water, bow first.

"Get in."

Gerhard put his mother in the stern. That part of the boat was closest to them, and she wouldn't have to put her feet into the water in the bottom of the boat. If she could keep her feet dry, the morning walk would be easier for her. He made his way to the bow. The boatman pushed off, jumped onto the stern to the middle seat. The oars were pulled out from under the gunwales and put in the oar locks.

He was slovenly, but he was also muscular. Gerhard had noticed the ease with which he had taken his place in the boat, and now he saw the man row the boat through the water rapidly and he did it with very little effort. Gerhard was sweating a little. That man could leave their bodies on the American bank and row himself home. He'd have the coat, the money, and the luggage. Without a gun Gerhard didn't think he'd be able to do much about it.

The sky was getting light pink by the time they reached the place on the opposite bank that marked the end of a little used path on the

American side of the river. The boat went stern first and Frau Dirks stepped ashore with her suitcase. Gerhard scrambled after her. To his immense relief, he got past the boatman without incident. His suitcase was twice as heavy as his mother's but they both were carrying the same thing, potatoes cleverly buried in clothing.

He took his mother by the arm and led her a few paces up the path and then spoke quietly. "Let's slide to one side for a minute or two. I don't trust the boatman. We'll wait until we are sure he hasn't alerted a reception committee for us."

From where they were standing, as they waited, they could see the river and they watched the row boat re-cross it. By the time the man reached the Russian side of the river, it had grown quite light and Dirks could see clearly. As the boatman pulled his rowboat up on to the shore, two Russian soldiers stepped out of the bushes where they had been hiding. One of them put a gun in the man's stomach and gave an order. The boatman put his hands on his head, turned and started walking back to his house. One soldier went with him, the other began systematically to smash the boat.

"Where he is going," Gerhard said to his mother, "he will soon wish he had that coat, but it won't be with him."

"What will they do with him, Gerhard?"

"Put him in a slave labor camp. He is very strong. They will get a lot out of him before they work him to death." He looked around, "I think it is safe to go on. If the man were playing both ends against the middle, I don't think the Russians would have picked him up."

She nodded. "He thought he took a coat for a boat ride, but he took a coat for his life." She turned and started walking up the path.

Gerhard followed her. His relationship with his mother was changing. He realized he'd spent most of his formative years in the company of his father. They had interests in common, and a genuine respect based on ability. He was beginning to see that his mother had both brains and guts. He felt that by the time their trip was completed, if it ever were, they would not only be mother and son, they would be friends.

FIVE

Corporal George Hovart and Private First Class Gary Sloane climbed into their jeep and prepared to go out on patrol. They had on their helmets, helmets with the large MP printed on the front of them, and the usual large sign was on the front of their vehicle, MILITARY POLICE.

As they pulled away from the headquarter's tent in Bad Lausic, Hovart mentioned that their duty wasn't too hard to take. "Riding around in a Jeep on a nice day in Spring, enjoying the sunshine. All we have to do is find some Heines too far from home."

"I'd rather be home in the States no matter what," Sloane remarked, "There's no place like home. How come the Germans don't feel that way? How come they're so anxious to get away from the Russians?"

"I've heard some stories. We don't talk about it much in our newspapers or anything, but the Russians aren't any different than the Nazis." Hovart, who was driving the jeep, turned down the small road leading to Ebersbach. The back roads were what the Germans used when they were trying to sneak west.

"You know, Lt. Bachman's family is from this area." Hovart continued, "And he speaks German real easy. He was talking the other night to the Captain when I was on desk duty. He was telling some stories he's heard from the local people about what's going on east of here and it didn't make for pretty listening. If the stories are anywhere near true, I'd be leaving for the West right along with 'em."

"How come we're Russia's allies then?"

"I don't know."

They rode in silence to Ebersbach and then took a small road west. In a couple of kilometers they saw a man and a woman walking ahead of them. Each had a suit case.

Hovart slowed the Jeep. "Here's a couple more."

They stopped the Jeep beside the two pedestrians and looked at them. The man was a good deal younger than the woman, they could be mother and son.

"Do you speak any English?" Hovart asked.

"A very little." The man was the one who answered.

"Your name?"

"Gerhard Dirks. This is my mother, Frau Dirks."

"What do you have in the suitcases?"

Gerhard pretended not to understand. "Suitcases?"

Hovart pointed at them. "What's in those things?"

"Ahh. Potatoes." The suitcases had been cleverly re-packed so it looked like the clothing was there to protect the food. The Russians would have stolen the potatoes if they had seen them, and the suitcases too, but Gerhard hoped Americans wouldn't. Gerhard waited patiently while the corporal looked at the opened suitcase.

"Who are those for?"

"I don't understand."

"Where are you going with potatoes?"

The memorized map of the area was in the front of Gerhard's mind and he answered easily. "We are taking food to relatives in PreiBnitz."

"Where are you from? Where's your home?"

Gerhard looked at the clean, shaven, baby face of the corporal. This was almost too easy. "We live in Ebersbach."

The corporal consulted his map. "Seven kilometers, Sloane, they're legal. Let's go."

Gerhard watched the Jeep disappear in the dust as it went down the road, closed his suitcase and prepared to walk west. The route he had planned was very devious. It went from town to town and each of the two towns was within a few kilometers of the other. It doubled the number of miles they would have to walk, but they were always legal. No matter where he was stopped along their way he would be going from point A to point B, and A and B would be close enough to each other to make their walk within the provisions of the military occupation.

Frau Dirks looked at her son in amazement.

She could not understand any English. "Weren't they Military Police?"

"Yes."

"How did you get rid of them?"

"I told them we were from Ebersbach and were going to PreiBnitz. Mama, some of these American Military Police speak German. If they try to talk to you, answer as little as possible. Let me do the talking if you can. I have the map in my head, and I always know where we are."

"You have lots of things in your head."

The sun was getting warmer and Gerhard no longer missed his coat. His mother was appreciating the warmth too; the night they had spent in a farmer's hay stack had been a little on the cold side. They walked with a certain urgency. They knew the rumors. The Americans might pull back and give the Russians some more of Germany. They wanted to get as far west as they could. Frau Dirks spoke again.

"I think God will see us home, Gerhard."

He smiled. "I hope so."

"You don't believe in God, do you Gerhard?"

The direct question surprised him, it was not characteristic of his mother to be that blunt, but their friendship was growing. Walking across central Europe together, they were like two people adrift in a life boat. He decided to be honest.

"No, Mama, I don't."

"Who not? You were raised to believe."

"Yes, I was interested as a child and I learned my catechism, but there are problems."

"What problems?"

"You know those punched cards I used at Skoda? I brought some home from time to time."

"Yes. They were for storing information."

"Right. Well, Mama, they are very clumsy. I have some ideas about storing information, I don't think we will need cards very much longer. I think information should be put on something by electro-magnetic impulse. You can put information on an iron nail with one magnet and take the information off again with another. That is the principle that will work some day, and I will develop it. We will store thousands of pieces of information on something that can be magnetized, and then we will go back and pull out what we want, I have ideas about that too. When I get to the West, I will develop these things, and I will be first."

As he spoke the obvious enthusiasm began to show through and he became animated as he talked. She watched him with interest. Her husband had often talked about their son and just how brilliant he was.

"Gerhard, what has this to do with God?"

"It says in the Bible that God will someday judge the world. Even worse, I remember reading in the Gospel something Jesus said about men having to explain every loose word they have ever spoken.

"Now, I know a little about data storage, about storing information and retrieving it. Where are you going to put a record of everything that every human being has ever done or said, and how, out of that material, could you possibly find what you're looking for? Worse, the Gospel talks about being judged about our secret thoughts—everything we've allowed to live in our minds.

"Mama, I want to see a data storage bank that has in it everything that every human being, since there were human beings, has done, said and thought. I don't care if you store it by moving atoms instead of molecules." Here he stopped short for a second. That was a pregnant thought, he'd have to work on that idea some day. "If it is only atoms, where could you store all that information? And how could you find what you wanted, when you wanted it? Such a concept boggles the mind, forget it. And if there is no judgment, how can you accept as true a story that has such a judgment as an intrinsic part?"

Gerhard paused for a moment and then continued. "In school once we had to read a play by an English author, Shakespeare. There was a line in the play that I have never forgotten. It applies to this judgeless world, 'sound and fun, signifying nothing, an idiot's delight.' That is the world we live in."

Anna was silent for a while. She wanted to frame her sentences carefully. When she did speak, she spoke in a slow and gentle way which contrasted completely with the harshness of his tone and the rapidity with which he had argued. "I cannot answer your argument, son." She had not called him that for years. "I would not try. Your father would not agree with you. He was an intelligent man and he believed that God had become man and lived among men as Jesus Christ. Your father believed and lived accordingly and he was not stupid."

"How did he like Hitler?" Gerhard asked with bitterness.

"At first he liked him very much. Hitler was bringing Germany out of chaos and into order. Your father was very pleased. Then things began to happen which were wrong and he began to work for the underground, not only endangering himself, but all of us. He didn't dare say anything to you."

Something that had happened in the past fit into place. "Herr Reinecker, was he in on it? The grey haired man who disappeared?"

"Yes. When he was taken, your father had a bad time, but Reinecker never talked and that was the end of your father's activity. He didn't know how to get in touch with the underground again."

Gerhard's blood ran cold as he thought of what might have happened. "Reinecker must have been killed. From what the Czechs told me, I would say that any man alive in the hands of the Gestapo talks."

"Maybe. Reinecker knew the Lord, too. Maybe he had someone helping him remain silent. Anyway, regardless of what you believe about 'data storage' they both are with the Lord now."

Gerhard could have kicked himself. It was one thing to have an intellectual argument about the existence of God. It was something else to chisel away at his mother's hope and comfort.

"Mama, let's talk about things we agree on. It's a beautiful day."

* * *

They walked for days, always with the mountains of Southern Germany on their left and rolling hills or flat lands on their right. They were stopped by American patrols twice more, but Gerhard had no problem with them. Always he was within the proper distance of two towns, the one toward which they were walking and the one behind in which he pretended to live.

One of the soldiers who questioned him was an American-German and spoke fluently in German. Gerhard would have had more trouble with him had he not been alert. It was Gerhard's practice to look closely at each town as they went through it, so that if he were questioned he would know the land marks. The soldier had been shrewder than most and had asked about places in the town Gerhard had just claimed as home. His memory served him well and he answered the soldier with apparent ease.

Anna Dirks had been able to follow the German conversation and was mystified. After the soldiers drove away, she asked her son about it.

"How did you know all that about the town we went through?"

"I looked and remembered."

"God gave me a very smart son, whether you believe in Him or not."

She had answered in an almost jovial mood, and Gerhard changed the subject. "Your knee, it does not seem to trouble you any more."

"No. It bothers me very little, although the arthritis is still there. Part of the trouble with my knee was my stomach. I ate too much and I weighed too much. I don't weigh too much any more. I'm down to where I could get into my wedding gown and find it too large. There's little strain on the knee, so the exercise is doing it good. How much farther do we have to go to reach my home?"

She meant Buttstadt, the town in which she had been born. Her name had been Anna Hennriette before she married Gerhard's father. Gerhard was familiar with the town. When his father had been drafted during the first world war, his mother had returned to her father's house with her son. Gerhard had gone to school for the first time in his life in Buttstadt.

"Borna and Zeitz are behind us. We have Eisenberg and Apolda and then we are within twenty kilometers of Buttstadt."

"It is only twelve kilometers from Apolda to Buttstadt, I remember."

"We cannot go direct. There would be more than eight kilometers between towns. We don't want to get caught so close to the end. We will go through Pfiffelbach and Oberreissen."

"There are not likely to be many patrols that far west."

"I don't expect any after Eisenberg, but we will take no chances."

"Do you want me to stay in Buttstadt?"

"I think it would be best, Mama. You know everyone in town and they know you, and the farmers know the trades people. There will be food and you will be with relatives who will watch out for you. I do not yet know what I will do in Langensalza, but I promise that if I go farther west, I will come back for you."

"That is good, Gerhard. This has been a hard walk for an old lady, but a good one, and a beautiful one since we crossed the Mulde." She pointed to the view of the hills to the south of them. "See how green. This has been one of the nicest springs ever. Also, getting to know you better has helped fill the hurt your father's death left." Her eyes filled with tears.

"It has been good to know you better, Mama, and I shall know you better still, someday."

"There is a drive in you, Gerhard, that will not be put to rest. You think it is inventions and machines, but that is only part. Someday you will make your peace with God. I know it." She saw him frown and added, "I promise that I will try never to mention it again until it has happened. All right?"

"All right, Mama."

She changed the subject. "What did you finally decide to do with your personal things, the things you had at Roztoky?"

"We decided to send them to Nebra. I have a relative there, and it is an out-of-the way place. When I have seen you safely to Buttstadt, I will walk up there and see if the things are safe. Then when something close to normalcy returns I can send them to wherever we decide to live."

The month of May had come and gone. Hitler had been officially declared dead, although nothing had been said over German radio about suicide. There were persistent rumors that a peace treaty with the Allies had been signed. At Apolda, the atmosphere was relaxed. The city was west of the Salle and south of the Undstrut rivers. No one felt that the Russian occupation would come that far west. The rumors that ran through the German population talked about a meeting at a place called Yalta on the Black Sea. The rumors were that all of East Europe would be handed to Joseph Stalin along with a small part of Germany. There had been uneasiness when the Americans had stopped at the Mulde and had dragged their feet until Russian forces "liberated" Berlin. But in 1945 no one believed for a moment that Stalin's grip would extend almost to Frankfurt, and that someday the Americans would let the Russians build a wall that would seal in the imprisoned people of Eastern Europe.

Things in Apolda were so close to "normal" that Gerhard abandoned his zig-zagging. In Apolda he met one of his in-laws. The man had a horse and wagon and he offered to drive it to Buttstadt and give them a ride, if Gerhard would ride in a wagon. Gerhard would. His mother had walked for weeks and had crossed the middle of Germany, but for the last twelve kilometers, she would ride.

* * *

Gerhard found his relative in Nebra. Gerhard's things had not arrived from Roztoky; not one of the crates had been seen. He checked back down the route of shipping as far as he could go, which was fewer and fewer kilometers as the Russian occupation constantly expanded. Twelve hours of searching turned up no information at all. That meant that some very valuable personal things were gone. Worse, it meant that some things that could under no circumstances be replaced were gone also. He had taken home movies of his children. Each child was photographed as it took its first steps. Such things can never again be reproduced, they are gone when they are gone. The loss of home, furniture, clothing and related things was hard to take, but he could start to work and accumulate again. The personal things were gone forever.

If the crates that had been shipped from his lab to Sommerda had arrived, he'd have something with which he could go to work, that and eighty thousand marks he and his mother had carried from Prague. That would be a start and he could begin to build again.

He walked south out of Nebra, crossing the Unstrut River and sticking to the main road. He had few worries. He was miles from the nearest Russian and the Americans were not keeping close watch. One thing was disquieting—there was an attitude of cooperation between the Russians and the Americans. The Americans did not see the danger. He shrugged his shoulders as he walked. Time would tell. Meanwhile, he had to get a job, get some income and rejoin his family.

At Sommerda he was delighted to find that his crates were there. Everything had arrived from the lab. He asked for Luce, the director of the facility at Sommerda. He wanted to arrange to go to work immediately. Herr Luce, he was informed, was no longer connected with the facility and was at his home, packing his things, preparing to leave the city. They would call Herr Luce and tell him that Dr. Dirks wished to speak to him.

Luce came back to the factory promptly to see Dirks; the two men had been acquainted for years. Like Dirks, Luce had lost weight and his clothes were shabby and ill-fitting. Gerhard felt they would be able to talk with some frankness and he was curious about Luce's move.

"I don't know what is behind it, Gerhard. Two days ago an American major from the Army of Occupation showed up here and told me to pack my things in crates he supplied and be ready to be moved within four days."

"Did he say where you were going?"

"Not a hint."

Gerhard looked at his friend for a moment. He

was convinced the man was not lying. "I hope they are not moving you east."

"I hope to God they're not, but I know nothing. I am only guessing. The officer was American. I'm going west. I would guess that they are getting ready to open subsidized manufacturing for the Allies and they are assembling those of us who are experienced in the kind of work they want to see developed."

Luce seemed kindly disposed and so Gerhard pushed him a little. "Could you include me in the group going?"

"No. I have no way of knowing who, if anybody is in charge. I wouldn't know where to start talking."

"Can you arrange for me to have a job here as you leave?"

"No. I have been told that I have absolutely no more authority."

"What are they going to do with this place?"

"As far as I know, nothing."

"What would you do if you were me?" Gerhard asked.

"Where's your family?"

"Bad Langensalza."

"Go join them, and good luck."

"Thank you." Gerhard turned and walked away. It wasn't far to Bad Langensalza.

The German branch of Power's was to be returned to Power's at the close of the war. Their corporate headquarters were in London and they were privy to much British intelligence. Also, they had good American connections; they were planning to become part of Remington Rand. Such people have inside information and frequently know what is to happen. They would say nothing to warn their German employees in Sommerda, but they were not about to rebuild or refurnish anything there. They had no plans to build or develop anything east of Frankfurt. They knew the terms of Yalta.

They did not know the inventions that were in the head of Gerhard Dirks. If they had, they would have moved a great deal to see that he joined Luce. They didn't know, and they left Gerhard in the East, walking toward Langensalza.

It was the 20th of June when he arrived to enjoy a glorious family reunion, not often duplicated in Germany in 1945. During July, Truman and Stalin were to meet in Potsdam with an aging and no longer competent Churchill for a conference that would ratify the agreement made by Roosevelt at Yalta. That agreement would change the history of Europe. As a very minor concomitance, it would also destroy the best laid plans of Gerhard Dirks.

SIX

First Lieutenant Howard Jones 0987005, U.S. Army was about as American as his name, except for one factor. His mother had been German and had spoken to him in that language from childhood. This ability to speak another language had landed Lt. Jones one of the best possible assignments. He was the ranking officer of the American Army of Occupation stationed at Bad Langensalza. There wasn't an officer who out-ranked him for miles in any direction. Under his command were three enlisted men and two vehicles, a Jeep and a G.I. truck. Better than that, he had thousands of Germans under him, all of whom seemed to be bent on fulfilling his every wish. Still, the assignment had its drawbacks.

As he got out of bed that August morning and looked in the mirror, he didn't like the face he saw. It was getting fat, and it was the face of a liar. Keeping his mouth shut about what he knew had been very hard indeed.

His corporal knocked on his door. "Lieutenant!"

"What is it?"

"There's a group of Krauts out here who want to talk to you."

Jones frowned. He was going to have to lie again, and he wasn't as good at it as he should be.

"I'll finish shaving and be out."

"Yes, sir."

Jones took his time. He was going to have to prepare himself to be convincing. He had received a sealed message via motorcycle messenger a week previously. It had been top secret, he was ordered to read it, burn it, and obey it. He was not to talk about its contents to anyone in his command nor to any German upon penalty of general court martial.

He finished shaving, combed his hair and put on his shirt and blouse. With his side arm in place he looked at himself in the mirror once more, and satisfied with everything except his expanding middle, he stepped out into the main room of the small house he occupied. It served as an office. On the far side of the corporal's desk a half dozen men stood and waited for him. He recognized the town baker, Hermann Konig, a good humored man with a wife, children and grandchildren. The man made some delicious but fattening strudel. Jones was going to miss it.

The baker stepped forward. "Herr Lieutenant, this is my son-in-law, Herr Doktor Gerhard Dirks. He has recently joined us."

"Another one who had made it out from under the Russians. Well, Herr Doktor," the lieutenant said to himself, "you didn't make it far enough."

Out loud he asked, "What is it, Herr Doktor?"

Gerhard noticed that the lieutenant's German was good, and he had a Berlin accent. "The Lieutenant speaks excellent German."

Jones was in no mood to spar. He was sure that the man in front of him knew all that the rest of the people in town knew about him, and that was plenty, but he repeated the sentence he'd spoken dozens of times.

"My mother's parents were from Berlin. We frequently spoke German in my home in Nebraska. Again, what is it, Herr Doktor?"

Gerhard plunged in, "There are persistent rumors to the effect that you will be leaving us shortly and that the Russians are coming here." He wasn't sure that "rumor" was a strong enough word. The moving of Herr Luce to the west was more than a rumor.

Jones had practiced his reply, he knew the question would be coming again and again, and he hoped he would sound convincing. It was strange that at that moment he should think of his father back in Nebraska. His father ran a mortuary and was able to talk to the bereaved in a way that made them think he really cared. Maybe, Jones thought now, his father really did care, maybe his sympathy wasn't all front. Jones knew that right at that moment he, Lt. Jones, would trade places with almost anyone, anywhere. He'd have to have a talk with his father when he got back to Nebraska.

"Dr. Dirks, these rumors are persistent, but I assure you that they are completely without foundation. I have been given orders and plans for the de-Nazification of this area. Now, why don't you gentlemen go on about your business."

Gerhard spoke once more. He wasn't sure the young man was telling the truth. It sounded rehearsed.

"Herr Lieutenant, I have seen the Russian Army enter a German city east of here. It was not a pleasant sight. Here in Langensalza we have wives, daughters, small children. We would be better off in the forest than in this town if the Russians are coming. If you know anything, say nothing further and we will run for our lives."

Jones knew what would happen to him if, when the Russian came, the German population had evacuated. There'd be hell to pay.

"Don't be foolish, there's nothing to run from." He turned to the baker, "Hermann, I'm late for breakfast this morning, but I'll be in tomorrow morning for some more strudel. You make it better than my grandmother."

"Thank you, Herr Lieutenant." Hermann Konig smiled, and turned to leave. The others followed. The bit about the strudel had been believable.

As soon as they left, Jones went back into his bedroom. He wanted to sit on the bed until he quit shaking. He thought that now he had a little insight into how Judas must have felt. Well, the Germans had been pretty brutal in their turn and they had started the damn war. They could just take the consequences.

Right on schedule, at 02:00 hours the next morning the Russian contingent showed up. They met the Americans on the outskirts of town. The Russian officer in command spoke German and he wished Jones good luck and dismissed him. Jones got into his jeep, driven by his corporal and started west. The other two G.I.'s followed in the truck.

The four Americans were replaced by twenty-five Russians: some disciplined soldiers, a couple of political officers and an officer from the NKVD. Road blocks were set up around the perimeter of the city and when they were in place, the rest of the Russian contingent walked into town quietly. They didn't take over a house on the edge of town, they moved into the main hotel. Once they were there, no one who went in came out.

* * *

Gerhard woke early. Gertrud was still sleeping. It was good to be with her again, and with the children. The three were growing so rapidly. It was a joy to watch them grow; these years would never come again. The two older children had firm pictures of him in their minds in spite of his absense. It was only with the youngest, Wolfgang, that he was having any trouble with rapport. The child was just past his second birthday, and the months that Gerhard had been gone had been important months. Also, Hermann, the child's grandfather had loved the boy on sight, and had taken a place in the child's heart that, under normal circumstances, would have been Gerhard's. But, the little one was coming around nicely and Gerhard was pleased.

He eased himself out of bed quietly and walked to the window to see if the morning was going to be cloudy or fair. He, Gertrud and the children had two rooms in the top of his father-in-law's house and the view from the window showed him half the town.

There was a small breath of wind and the flag that had been hanging unnoticed from the flag pole over the hotel moved and showed itself. Gerhard swore, waking his wife.

"What is it Gerhard? What has happened?"

He pointed and she came to the window to join him. It was there, the hammer and sickle on a background of red: red like blood.

"So, Gertrud, that Lieutenant Jones was lying in his teeth and we are rats in a trap."

* * *

As nearly as Gerhard could tell, every man in Bad Langensalza was in the school house, every man under sixty years of age. The Russians hadn't missed anyone. They had surrounded the town and then gone house to house. There was no escape, for there was not only the physical search of the city, there were also lists. The local German Communists had compiled a listing for the Russians, one that showed the residents of every house in the city, and a separate listing of the men under sixty. Gerhard watched the German and the Russian Communists. The Germans were treated with a mild and ironic contempt by their Russian superiors. Gerhard was confident that the Germans were in no way aware of this contempt. He knew the Russians were not fools and they knew that very few men in Germany who could fit into the German culture successfully would bother being Communist. Gerhard knew that there were dedicated German Communists, men who staked their lives on their faith, but such Communists were not in Bad Langensalza. Here, the Communists were the malcontents, the discontents, those who could not reach the level of society that they considered equal to their "abilities." Regardless of what they were or what they had been, they were now useful to the Russians and dangerous to everyone else. For the first time in their lives these people had high sounding titles and felt important. They didn't want any other German to miss the point.

One by one, the men were called out of the main room for interrogation. The Russian political officer and the man from the NKVD were doing the questioning in two small rooms that had served as office for the administration of the school. The rooms were not now being used for administrative purposes, the school was closed. So was the bank. That was the first thing the Russians had done the day they arrived. They locked the bank. The remainder of Gerhard's eighty thousand marks were on their way to Moscow. It wasn't only that they wanted the money, but they knew that without money, mobility and opportunity are restricted, and control is increased.

By two in the afternoon, Gerhard was called. He went, half sick with hunger, fear and the uncertainty of it all. He knew that if the political officer could find out what Gerhard knew about data access and transmission and about certain computing techniques that had military value, Gerhard would disappear into Russia and never see his family again.

As he walked down the hall to the appointed office, he could see out a window to the school yard. The women and children of Bad Langensalza had formed a ring around the school building and since eight that morning they had been crying and calling out and pleading with the Russians to turn the men loose. In the few seconds that he had to look through the window he didn't see any of his family but he knew that they were there too.

Inside the office, the Russian political officer sat at what had been the principal's desk looking at a handful of papers. There was a German Communist standing beside him with a smug look on his face. Gerhard recognized him as the janitor of the city hall. Now he was mayor of Bad Langensalza. There was an empty, straight-backed chair in front of the desk, and without being asked, Gerhard took it. On the wall behind the Russian there was a picture of Joseph Stalin staring down on them both. The political officer spoke.

"You did not wait to be asked to sit down."

"I did only what I thought was expected of me."

The Russian continued looking at the papers in

his hands for a moment before he spoke again. "I see that you call yourself Gerhard Dirks. What happened to the 'Herr Doktor'?"

"Under the circumstances, it seemed pretentious." Not too good an answer, but the best he could do. It had not been wise to leave off his degree when he filled out his form. This Russian might know a great deal. Gerhard would stick to the truth.

"What field of study gave you a Doktorate?"

"Law."

"Where?"

"University of Leipzig." So far so good. Law was a long way from computer controlled armament production.

"Were you a member of the Nazi party?"

"Yes."

"Your candor is refreshing. The membership in the Nazi party seems to have diminished to almost nothing in the past few weeks." He looked up from the papers in his hand and met Gerhard's gaze for the first time. Gerhard recognized the look in the man's eyes. He'd seen the same ice cold, almost inhuman stare when he'd been face to face with some of the S.S.

"Tell me, Dirks, what have you been doing for the good of the people since you returned here?"

"I have been building rectifiers."

"I'm not familiar with this. What is it for?"

Gerhard spoke more easily, he was on home turf. "I know that right now, there are no more batteries for autos and trucks being built. The old ones have to be made to do. Also what we have to use for fuel makes cars and trucks hard to start and puts still more strain on the tired batteries. So the batteries have to be charged frequently. The battery is direct current electricity and the house or garage is alternating current. A rectifier is a device that changes the direction of every other pulse, so that the current flows only one way. Then you can plug the rectifier into a house current and put direct current into the battery. Then the battery will start the truck."

"Where did you get the parts for these?"

"At the war surplus depot on the edge of town. There are all kinds of things there, and I bought what I needed to make rectifiers." He didn't add that if he had known that they were going to steal his bank account he would have spent a lot more money on parts.

"Do you put these together by yourself?"

"Yes." Gerhard sensed that this question was important. "I do all the labor."

The Russian turned to the local Communist for confirmation and Gerhard held his breath. If this man failed to confirm, Gerhard was dead.

The German nodded agreement and Gerhard began to breath again.

"To whom do you sell these?"

Gerhard felt that this was another important question. "I haven't sold any. I have used one to keep my father-in-law's truck going. He is a baker."

He saw a slight frown cross the face of his interrogater and he realized he hadn't been asked what his father-in-law did, he was volunteering information which could be taken as a lack of fear. He must be careful to answer only what he was asked. He wasn't asked anything more and he sat and sweated. After what seemed like a very long time the Russian spoke again.

"Report to room number three."

"Yes, sir."

Gerhard rose and left. Room three was about half full of men who had been questioned. Sitting there was Hermann. They took hold of each other.

"Wherever we're going," Gerhard pointed out, "We're going together."

"I'm worried about Heinz. I hope we see him too." Heinz was Gertrud's brother and the only son of Hermann. He worked in the bakery and still lived at home.

"Don't be too insistent on that. If we are being shipped east, it is better that one of us is left behind with the families."

In another hour Heinz joined them. There was subdued rejoicing. Then there was more waiting, until dark. When it was dark, the men in rooms two, three and four were sent home. The reason for the Russians waiting until dark to release the men became apparent later. No one ever saw what happened to the men in room number one. No one ever saw or heard from any one of them again. They disappeared from the face of the earth.

* * *

A couple of days after the interrogation in the

school building, Gerhard and his men relatives held an evening meeting in the bakery trying to figure things out. So far, none of them had been taken. Why? Why had those who had been taken been the ones chosen? There was no pattern.

It was Dirks who saw it first. He brought his hand down on the table in front of him.

"That's the pattern—no pattern! Look!" Now that he saw what was going on, he spoke excitedly. "If they took all Party members, then everyone who was a Party member would know that he was going to be picked up, sooner or later. That would mean that someone not a Party member would feel safe. Instead, they take some and leave some."

He pointed his finger at Hermann.

"Think, is there any part of our community that has not been touched? They chose with great care. No one is safe, and it is this uncertainty that they want. Uncertainty breeds fear."

Gerhard was right. Uncertainty did breed fear, and it entered the community like a brown fog creeping into nooks and crannies. It was not long until they had what all Germans call "The East German Look." It is a refusal to look someone in the eye for long, and a constant turning of the head in effort to see if anyone is listening.

* * *

The Konig bakery was one of the favorite "gathering" places in Langensalza. The pastry was good, even if it wasn't up to pre-war standards. Hermann couldn't get all the ingredients he wanted, but he did have good contacts with the local farmers and he got most of the staples in adequate supply. In the back of his store he had his kitchen with its ovens. The front of the building had display cases filled with baked goods, and a dozen small tables at which customers sat, ate, drank and gossiped. It had been a popular place for years, particularly with the German soldiers when they had come home on leave. After the Americans came, they were there frequently, and the four Americans had mixed with the locals.

When the Russians came, they took the place over completely every morning. Few of the locals cared to mix, and except for the Communist sympathizers, the morning's conversation was in Russian. Gerhard worked for his father-in-law during the morning rush. He was needed. The baking for the day had to be done, and the early morning customers had to be waited on. Gertrud's niece worked there too. She was a pretty girl, Bavarian to the core, blonde, braided hair, blue eyes, a husky, good-looking girl. Gerhard was happy to have her call him "Uncle." She had worked in the bakery since she had turned ten. She was now 18, and had worked for eight years.

During those eight years, as she had grown older, she had learned how to reject advances from men in general and soldiers in particular, polite ones and impolite, and she had learned how to take care of herself. She could reject without offending. Her boy friend, if he ever got back to Langensalza, would be her fiancé. However, she had had no experience with the Gestapo or the NKVD. Gerhard knew what was involved in such contacts and when he came out of the kitchen with a tray full of baked goods, he was upset to see his niece engaged in a friendly conversation, in German, with the Russian who had the marking on his collar that showed he was a member of the Russian secret police. Gerhard wasn't sure that his niece knew the meaning of the Russian ensignia, and she was chatting away merrily with the man.

Gerhard got as close to them as he could, hoping he'd find an opportunity to interject himself into the conversation. The opportunity never came. The man's proposition did. It was delivered in a cold and straightforward manner.

There was a slang expression the Bavarian Germans used about that kind of an approach. It was related to the German word for pig, and it meant that the man was in too big a hurry to get what he wanted. Gerhard heard his niece use it. His blood ran cold and he started to sweat.

The Russian let out a sentence in his own language that did not sound friendly. Then in German he asked, "What did you call me?"

He spoke loudly and the room was suddenly silent. There was something in his eyes, and the girl suddenly sensed danger. She began to apologize and to try to explain that it was a phrase that was used jokingly. She got nowhere and sensed that too. She started to stammer and then to blubber. The NKVD officer said nothing, he just stared at her. Gerhard felt himself getting sick. Finally the officer turned on his heel and walked out of the bakery. The girl ran for the kitchen. Gerhard set his tray down and leaned against the wall. He made up his mind yet again to get to the West. His daughter Ingrid would never be raised in this atmosphere, no matter what he had to do.

SAN FRANCISCO, CALIFORNIA. Marybelle Dirks, a member of the teaching staff at the Stanford School of Nursing, married Gerhard several years after his first wife Gertrud died of cancer. She gives her husband an affectionate look as he speaks passionately of his conviction that what happened in Germany could also happen here.

"People think that a dictatorship forces things down on the oppressed. This is not true, and it is not the way things worked. The evil is not forced down. It is sucked down, by the opportunists among the oppressed.

"When the Communists take over a city, they put in some of their own very competent people. Then these competent appoint the grossly incompetent. They take a man of no education and no training, a Communist national, and they say 'You are mayor.' They pay him the mayor's salary and put him in the mayor's villa. Then they take someone else, maybe someone out of jail, and they say, 'you are the new chief of police.' Then they point out to these men and their friends that they never had it so good before. They are right.

"Pretty soon the city does not run well. Pretty soon the police department isn't functioning; they don't know what to do. You cannot argue with them,

they have not the intelligence necessary to argue, they just hit you if you ask an uncomfortable question. Soon they are desperate. They don't want to lose their new positions, so what can they do?

"They go to the one who appointed them and say 'What do we do?' Now this is what the new authorities are waiting for. The man who appointed the incompetent now tells them what to do. The orders of the dictatorship are carried out willingly by the incompetents that have been appointed. They are kept in power through fear.

"I see this same sort of thing going on, even in the United States. Whenever someone, anyone with political power, for political reasons, appoints someone who would not otherwise be considered for the job, the person doing the appointing has increased his own power. The person appointed will do whatever he or she is told to do. You can rule a whole country with an iron fist by appointing people who will do anything to stay in office, but don't really know what they are doing.

"I don't know that this can be prevented, but one thing slows it down. It is the genius of the American system of balance of powers that keeps things within certain bounds. The leaders from one branch of government can object to people grossly out of place and incompetent in another branch. As long as America's political power is divided evenly between three branches of government things may not get out of hand in this area.

"One thing does trouble me, though. Communists, and all dictatorships for that matter, use

paperwork and red tape to control things. You have to have a permit for everything. I see this growing in this country at an alarming rate. To build something, to do something, to operate something, you fill out more and more forms, more and more papers. Bureaucrats keep themselves in office better than politicians, and bureaucracy in this country is growing in an alarming way. It will be a tool for someone to come along and use. It can spell disaster."

SEVEN

The official announcement had said that anyone who wished to establish the fact that they had a West Berlin residence would have to register with the authorities in Berlin before the end of September. That meant travel and travel meant hardship. Train service was not good.

The Russians had announced that Germany had twice as much in the way of rail transportation as was really needed. (This may have been true according to Russian standards.) So, the conquerers helped themselves to half the locomotives still running, half the railway cars, but worse, they took every other track. They pulled them up with slave labor and shipped them to Russia.

This meant that where there were four tracks, two were taken and the fourth had to be moved to make the first useable. The work was extensive and the train service limited. When Gerhard and Gertrud got on the train for Berlin there were half as many cars as there should have been, and twice as many people. Their car was packed solidly with humanity. People sat on the seats, on their baggage and on each other. Still others stood in the cracks.

Gerhard and Gertrud had no problem getting permission to go to Berlin. They could show an apartment address in that city that had been theirs for years. More important, they could leave hostages in Langensalza, three children and the grandparents. The local Communists knew they would come back.

The Dirkses were among the more fortunate, they had a pair of seats. Gertrud sat next to the door of the compartment, the door through which entrance and exit was made when the train was stopped. The train left the station an hour late and they began the most uncomfortable journey of their lives.

*   *   *

Mrs. Schneider met them at the door of their apartment. She was not glad to see them. They might want some of their apartment back, and that meant that someone else would have to move out. Gerhard put her mind to rest somewhat when he explained that their visit would be brief. At this point, she gave him a message. Herr Kostka, the man he had asked about, had been discharged from the army and had come looking for Gerhard. Frau Schneider had the note he had left. She found it and handed it to Gerhard.

It told Gerhard that Kostka was back in the same house, and that if Gerhard came back to Berlin, Kostka would be very happy to see him. Would he please look up his old friend?

Gerhard was delighted. He wanted to see Kostka. After explaining to Frau Schneider that they would be back that evening and would sleep on the living room floor, they took their leave. Gerhard took one of their suitcases with him.

They found Kostka; he was sharing the small house with another man who was not at home when the Dirkses arrived. Kostka had an advantage over Gerhard. Gerhard had been a nominal member of the Nazi party. He would find it easier to be "de-Nazified" than those who had been active in the party, but Kostka had not been in the party at any level at all. Consequently he had privileges that were not open to Dirks. He understood Dirks' position and circumstances and he was a friend. He would help if he could.

"I know what things are like at your apartment, I have met Frau Schneider. I wish I could offer you room here, but the man I share this place with comes home in the evening and he frequently has someone with him. You can come here to eat, though, during the day. Do you have food stamps?"

"Yes. I picked up some when I was in Berlin with my mother before the Russians came. On the basis of the same apartment address, I can get more."

He opened the suitcase he had brought with him, and pulled out one of four rectifiers. He handed it to Kostka.

"Could you sell this?"

"Yes, for a great deal, but why me?" Then he

remembered, Gerhard couldn't sell anything until he'd been de-Nazified. "I remember, now, you were a member of the Party. What's your status?"

"I can be only a common laborer until I'm de-Nazified. Because I was only a nominal member, they will clear me when they get to me, but there is so much paperwork, it could take up to three years."

"How many of these rectifiers do you have?"

"I brought four this trip, but I can make many more."

Kostka turned the rectifiers around in his hand slowly, looking at them carefully. "You have done a good job, Gerhard. Where did you get the materials?"

"A war surplus dump near Langensalza."

The two men were seated in the main room of the little house, sitting across from each other. Gertrud sat to one side and listened. She turned her head from side to side to see if anyone else was listening. Then she remembered that she was in West Berlin and didn't have to do that. Something inside of her relaxed a little.

"You want me to sell these." He looked at Gerhard, "They will bring a good price."

"Yes, and give me two-thirds of the money. Also I will register as a common laborer, working for you. You register as an employer. The money you get for the rectifiers you give to me as hourly wages. This gives me a cover in Langensalza. If I'm asked where I sell these, I don't sell them. I work for a man in Berlin named Kostka who pays me hourly wages."

"That work will not count here in Berlin."

"I know. I will get a job here too. Sometimes I will be working in Berlin, sometimes in Langensalza. I will be able to get my labor out of the way and work for Power's again."

"How will you get your family out of Langensalza?"

Gerhard knew better than to reveal any of the plan that was forming in his mind. "That remains to be seen."

Kostka held the rectifier up in his hand. "For me, this is a bargain. I will sell these today. The only suggestion I would make would be that you not trust your previous food stamp registration. Are you registered in Langensalza?"

"Gertrud is. She was there first with the children. I have not registered since the last time in Berlin."

"Register again, but only under your own name. Your name will be on the list in Berlin and Gertrud's on the list in Langensalza. That way, if they check, and they may, the same name will not appear twice."

"Thank you. It is agreed?"

"It is agreed. I am now an employer."

* * *

The train ride back to Langensalza was as bad as the ride to Berlin. Gerhard made up his mind that he would not take Gertrud any more, not unless the trains improved. Whenever he was in Berlin, he would be there alone. Under present conditions the trip was not fit for a woman. Not fit for a man either for that matter, it was fit only for cattle. He told Hermann and Heinz about it the day he returned to Langensalza. They were sitting around one of the small bakery tables after the place had been closed, enjoying a beer and chatting.

Hermann shook his head affirmatively, and anxiety showed on his face. "Things are not good here either, Gerhard. While you have been gone more people have disappeared. It was like you said, it could happen to anybody, but lately we've noticed a pattern. Now, the person who disappears is chosen from among those who have said something." Even as he spoke he looked around the closed bakery to be sure no one was listening. "Everywhere there are ears. They add people to every payroll, usually placing them in the personnel department so they can move others around. They even added someone here. That girl who worked here today. She came looking for a job on the basis of old friendship. Her father and I had been acquainted before he died. I gave the job, unsuspecting. Then Heinz saw her late one evening coming out of their headquarters. I sweated for an hour thinking back over everything that had been said in front of her. Fortunately, I don't think any of us slipped, or maybe we wouldn't be here.

"They have added teachers at the schools, one for each level. They teach the children propaganda.

They also show up at the teachers' meetings, and in the teachers' lunch room. They slide in and out like greased eels."

Hermann took another swallow of his beer and continued. "Two of the school teachers are among the missing. We discussed it at some length. Each of them had made some almost harmless remark about the occupation before they disappeared, but it is so uncertain. Others have said something and not disappeared. Even children. The child may say something on the play ground. It is a reflection of something heard at home, carelessly repeated. Another child whose parents are Communists hears it. You never see the child who talked again, maybe."

Gerhard suddenly felt a lump in his stomach. His son, Rainer, would be going to school very soon. The boy must be warned. It would be good to permit no talking about anything significant even in the family. Then there would be no slip. A child cannot repeat what he has not heard. Gerhard groaned.

"What a way to raise a family!" he thought in dismay.

* * *

Gerhard returned to Berlin in two more weeks with another three rectifiers. Kostka was glad to see him and had news. There was a rumor of labor openings. Everyone wanted jobs, but for manual labor jobs, ex-Party members sometimes had priority.

Gerhard took no chances. He was at the office

of employment early the next morning, hours before it opened. Even so, there were a hundred or so men ahead of him, waiting in line. By nine, the line began to move, slowly. By eleven he was inside the building and could hear the questions being put to the men who were ahead of him. He could also study the men doing the questioning. They all had one thing in common—they had been anti-Nazis, or they had been people who had suffered at the hands of the Nazis. This was a prerequisite for any German who wanted to go to work for the Army of occupation in any kind of a job.

Finally, it was Gerhard's turn at one of the desks.

"Your name?"

"Herr Doktor Gerhard H. Dirks."

"Were you a member of the Nazi party?"

"Yes."

"Which classification?"

"Four." That meant he had been a nominal member only.

"What did you do during the war?"

"I was in charge of cost control at the Skoda works, and production control at Prague."

The man questioning him was suddenly interested and he looked at Gerhard as though he was seeing him, really seeing him for the first time. "You have a Berlin address?"

"Yes." Gerhard showed his papers.

The man had a gleam in his eye that Gerhard didn't like. He spoke with noticeable sarcasm in his voice. "You now have a job." He scribbled on a pad, tore off the page and handed it to Dirks. "Report tomorrow morning at that address. You will be told what to do."

He had been given a job, one that would qualify for the de-Nazification program. Every weekend, until de-Nazification, Herr Doktor Gerhard H. Dirks was to be a garbage collector.

He had been given his slip on Friday, the next morning was Saturday and he reported for work. It was a dump, a garbage dump to which he reported. In back of the facility there were twelve beat-up, worn-out trucks. By six in the morning, there were also forty-eight Germans standing there waiting to be told what to do.

At exactly six another German employee of the Army of Occupation arrived in a Jeep. He had a handful of papers. Gerhard was standing closest to the man as he started to talk, and was handed the papers.

The man spoke in a harsh voice. "There are twelve sheets, one for each truck. The sheet contains a map and shows where each truck goes to pick up garbage. There are also forty-eight slips of paper. Put your name and the date on it. Divide yourselves into groups of four." He held up four fingers and counted out loud as though he were talking to imbeciles, "Ein, zwei, drei, vier. Take turns driving. One man drives, three pick up garbage."

Gerhard spoke up. "Excuse me, please. With what do we pick up the garbage?"

The man looked Dirks square in the eye. "With

your hands, you dirty, stinking, Nazi scum." He raised his voice to an even higher pitch. "Now get these trucks moving." He turned on his heel and walked away.

Gerhard kept one of the maps and one of the slips for himself. Three men attached themselves to him and gave him their names. Herr Bauer, who had been president of a bank in Potsdam, Herr Beyer who had been principal of one of the better high schools in Berlin and Herr Bietenhard who had been an executive in the Berlin Telephone Service. All of them were "class four," nominal members of the Nazi party.

"This is terrible work," Gerhard said. "But excellent company. Only the best people get these jobs."

The three others smiled, and Beyer spoke. "There is an old vaudeville joke about the country bumpkin who came to the big city and was given a job. Garbage man, five marks a day and all he could eat."

The others chuckled, might as well put a good face on the matter. Bauer spoke, apologetically. "I know this sounds like an excuse, but I do have a bad back." He pointed to the area near his sciatic nerve. "If I have to bend over and pick things up, I won't last long."

Gerhard looked at the truck. "If you can start that and keep it running, you will do your share. It's all right with me."

The others agreed and they went to work. In spite of the rotten job, and the stinking things they handled, there was rapport. It was one of the few times in Gerhard's life where he was accepted wholeheartedly as one of a group. He was to remember it with ironic amusement all the rest of his life.

* * *

For two years, Gerhard collected garbage in Berlin on the weekends. During the week he built rectifiers and lived under the Communist occupation in Langensalza. There were problems. There were no rules.

First there were those who disappeared, apparently at random selection. If someone disappeared it was not wise to ever mention the name again. For de-humanizing reasons, the Communists wanted the disappearance of a friend or neighbor treated as though it were something unworthy of note. If you mentioned the name of someone who was missing, you might be the next person missing. It did not work every time. If when you mentioned the name of the departed you always disappeared the air of uncertainty would be mitigated. It was one more of their ruleless rules.

Then there were the "round ups." For one reason or another, all men of certain ages would be required to report to, or be shipped to, another town to be registered. No one ever knew on those occasions who would and who would not return to his home. Gerhard cleverly avoided these forced assemblies.

On one occasion he lived in the forest for three days. He almost got caught. Some Russians with dogs were out hunting. There were deer in the forest and they made good eating because meat was scarce. Neither the Russians nor the dogs found Gerhard; he had buried himself under a large pile of brush and tree limbs.

Another time, while escaping from a forced assembly, he walked into a Russian machine gun, which had been set up to catch deserters. A Russian soldier escorted him back to the town, the town of Kleinberndten. Once back in the center of Kleinberndten, in a group of men milling around in the town square he watched for his chance and slipped away. He found a hay loft and buried himself in it. They didn't catch him a second time.

But he was worrying. He didn't believe his luck could hold up forever. Sooner or later, the Russians would get him, or one of his family. The strain was taking its toll—he was getting increasingly irritable and he was losing weight. The gut level drive to get himself and his family to freedom was eating at him constantly. Up to three years was a long time. Under the Russians it could be a very long time and it could be three years until, in the terms of the West, he would be de-Nazified.

It was at the end of his second year that the first ray of hope appeared. Men were disappearing off the garbage detail, without mentioning being de-Nazified. In a Russian zone, a disappearance would have been common place and unmentionable, but in Southwest Berlin it was noticeable.

He talked to Kostka about it one Sunday evening while they were having a bite to eat. Gerhard had stayed with his friend that particular weekend, instead of sleeping on the floor in the living room of his own apartment. Kostka's renter had left Berlin for a few days and Gerhard had been invited to take his place. It was in the fall of 1947, and in the Nikolassee district of Southwest Berlin, there were all kinds of luxuries restored. Gerhard had had a bath before supper; the utilities were beginning to work with pre-war efficiency.

"Where do they go, Kostka, these men who disappear?"

"I was wondering if I should mention it to you. I didn't want to give you false hopes, but it seems that men who find jobs other than labor are able to take them without too many questions being asked, even if they are not yet de-Nazified. If you are doing something else and are asked if you were a member of the Party, say you were not. No one is checking records like they used to, particularly not the Americans."

"Where could I get a job?"

"I ran across your friend Huth. He is back in Berlin and I spoke to him. They have opened up their business machines office again. Their headquarters are in Frankfurt, but they are keeping a representation in Berlin and are part of Remington Rand now. That American company bought several European firms including Torpedo in Frankfurt."

"Why would they buy Torpedo? What did they do?"

"Simple. They got their factory in Frankfurt through the war without having it bombed. Remington Rand wanted their name and their facility."

"I hope Becker came back too." Gerhard had things on his mind that only a technical man would understand and Becker was a good technician. Huth, on the other hand, was strong in the field of commercial applications. If he could talk to the two men at the same time, he was sure he could interest Remington Rand in what he wanted to develop.

The next morning, Gerhard went to the train that he usually took to get back to Langensalza. He kept looking for a familiar face among those boarding the train. Finally he found one, a man from Langensalza who had been in Berlin for a while. Gerhard gave him a message, telling him to leave it at the bakery, discreetly. Dirks would return to Langensalza one week late. If he had not sent the message, Gertrud would have worried herself to death. People who failed to come when they were supposed to, rarely came at all.

From the station, he went back to Nikolassee pondering the problem of paper. He had one clean, white sheet back in the apartment that had been tucked away inadvertently before the war started. If there was more paper in Berlin, it wasn't easily available to him. Then he got an idea. Instead of going to the apartment, he turned and walked under the autobahn and out to the lake at Wannsee. The lake shore was smooth, white sand.

At the edge of the lake he began to draw in the sand. Bent over, he worked for hours, putting down what had been developing in the back of his mind for years. When he was through, he had designed a rotating magnetic memory with track-selection by moveable head.

Back at the apartment, he took his one, large piece of paper and folded it carefully twice. With a very sharp kitchen knife he sliced along the folds and left himself with four pieces of paper. On one piece, with pen and ruler, he carefully reproduced what he had worked out on the sand.

The next day, he went back to the beach and worked for eight hours without stopping. His back ached, but he had what he wanted. He went back to the apartment and made his second drawing. It was a start-stop magnetic digital tape for sorting and transfer to matrix-storage. At the end of the third day he made his third drawing—a circuitry making possible the transfer of data from electronic matrix storage into tapes, discs and printers. His fourth drawing made possible the serial transfer from storage into matrix storage and parallel transfer into printers and display devices. Together the four pieces of paper laid the foundation for the development of computer technology for decades to come. The documents, showing design, drawing and description, were extremely valuable.

Friday, he went looking for Huth. He found him in the same office that had been Power's before the occupation. It was not the same girl at the desk. He had half expected it to be. This woman was older.

"Yes?" There was little respect in her greeting. Gerhard looked pretty dowdy.

"I'm Gerhard Dirks, I would like to see Herr Huth."

The woman's attitude changed abruptly. "I've heard them mention your name. I will be right back."

She went into the next room for a moment and when she came out she was closely followed by Huth. He extended his hand.

"Gerhard, so good to see you again. What have you been doing?"

"Collecting garbage."

Huth withdrew his hand. A little more coolly he said, "What can I do for you?"

"Is Herr Becker here?"

"Yes."

"I have some ideas. May I speak to you both?"

Huth was interested again. "Certainly, come in." He raised his voice, "Becker, please come into my office."

Becker greeted Gerhard with less enthusiasm than Huth had shown. There is always a certain reluctance to spend too much time with someone who can do your job better than you can, and might some day want your job. Gerhard knew he'd have to clear the air on that point to get Becker's complete cooperation. He was in a position to do that, as Gerhard was interested only in working alone. He changed the subject for a moment to satisfy his curiousity.

"The girl who was here. Do you know where she is?"

"No." Huth answered. "We have not seen her since we left for Frankfurt." He pointed to a chair. "Have a seat."

"Did she live on the East side of the city?"

"I'm afraid so."

"I hope for her sake she's dead."

"Don't be too hard on the Commies." Huth was a man with mixed loyalties. His father was German and so was his citizenship, but his mother had been English and he had gone to school in London. He tended to have a British point of view about some things, and now he was free to express it.

Gerhard raised his eyebrows. "Why not?"

"Well, you know it was no pleasure living under the Nazi Germans either. Ask any Jew."

"The things that were done—no, the things we did, for we all had a part in it, were terrible. We didn't know all we know now, or we'd have done things differently, but I'm sure that living under a government that tortures minorities is not a good place to live. However, it is no better to live under a government that tortures everybody and anybody."

Huth was mollified, first by Gerhard's admission of guilt and then by the weight of the argument. "You didn't come to talk politics; what is it?"

"I have, now, four inventions: rotating magnetic memories with track-selection by movable heads; start-stop magnetic digital tapes for sorting and transfer to matrix-storage; transfer from magnetic matrix storage into tapes, discs and printers; serial transfer from storage into matrix storage and parallel transfer into printers and display devices."

Becker was stunned. "Where do you have these?"

"On paper."

"There wouldn't be any chance of seeing anything?"

"No."

"Can't say that I blame you. If what you say you have, you have, everything we are even trying to design is now obsolete. Can you talk to me in general terms, without revealing too much?"

Gerhard did and Becker was soon convinced. Also, he was no longer worried about his position. Dirks was over his job like a kite. Better for Becker to ingratiate himself with Dirks. He turned to Huth.

"We've got to have these. We'll be way ahead of the entire industry."

That was enough for Huth. "All right, Gerhard, what do you want?"

"I want to get myself and my family out of Communist territory."

"Gerhard, you know we can't do that, it's too late."

"You can help."

"How?"

"To start with, you can give me a job."

Huth saw a bargaining point and began to use it. "I couldn't put you on the payroll unless I could justify it to the company by showing them something of what you have. For that, you'd have to trust me."

Gerhard was prepared for this. "I don't want to be on the payroll. Not for any appreciable amount. I want to be on your records as a hired consultant. The renumeration will be confidential, ten marks a year and I'll pay that to you myself."

Huth realized that Dirks wanted to keep sole possession of his inventions, and that somehow he intended to acquire the enabling capital. He was going to have to leave Dirks with the feeling that Remington Rand would be happy to settle for manufacturing and distribution rights. He smiled. "We'll pay you ten marks a year. What else?"

"I need permission to move myself and my family from West Berlin to Frankfurt. You are transferring me from the Berlin office to the Frankfurt office."

"But your family is not in West Berlin."

"That's my problem and I'll solve it."

Huth pursed his lips. He was playing a game that was dangerous, and he was playing against a man who had been thinking out the moves for years. He'd have dropped the whole matter if it hadn't been for the size of the stakes. Becker had signalled him that Dirks had what they were looking for. Both men knew that the future of the computer industry was in America. They had talked several times about how they might get there. The method was now available. If they could get their hands on what Dirks had done, it would mean two passports to the United States.

"I can give you the paper work, Gerhard, but where do you live when you get to Frankfurt? I cannot move you from Berlin to any German city without showing that you have a place to live when you get there."

"Do you know the street address of the Torpedo factory?"

"Yes."

"Use it."

Huth was getting uncomfortable and he looked at Becker. The technical man answered his look with a statement. He too was thinking about a passport to America. "I think we should give him anything he asks for, anything that we can grant, even if there are risks."

Gerhard looked at him. "Thank you." He said it sincerely, just as though he didn't know what was really on their minds.

Huth nodded his agreement. "All right." He turned to Gerhard, "Give us the total of what you want, the whole package. This business of hearing it bit by bit is a little like the Chinese water torture."

After the words were out, he realized he shouldn't have said "torture." That word was on everyone's mind these days.

Gerhard summed things up. "I need an order to

ship things to Berlin, no mention of people, just materials. Date it for four weeks from now. Then I need an employment transfer and orders to move five people from Berlin to Frankfurt. Date those six weeks from now. For my Berlin address, use my apartment. For Frankfurt, use the address of the Torpedo Factory."

Huth searched his memory. "You, your wife and three children make five. Your mother has the same name, you could move her. Don't you want six?" He spoke delicately, "Perhaps she has passed on?"

"No. She hasn't, but I will take care of her separately."

Huth stood up. "It is agreed. How soon do you need the papers?"

"I will be back for them in two or three weeks." Gerhard and Becker also rose from their chairs.

Dirks shook hands with both of them and took his leave. Inside, his emotions were playing havoc with his stomach. Hope surged forward, but fear followed on its heels.

EIGHT

In Bad Langensalza, Gerhard was not in as much danger as he thought. There was no way for him to find this out, but two of his rectifiers had found their way into Russian hands. One of them had found its way back to Langensalza and some of the Russian vehicles were using batteries that would have been useless without Gerhard's ingenuity. The Russians weren't about to tell Gerhard this, as it was in their interests to leave him with the same cold terror in his stomach that was common to the German population in general. Also, the protection was as thin as tissue paper. At the slightest hint of dissatisfaction with the conquerors, Dirks would disappear into the bowels of Russia just as fast as anyone else, rectifiers or no rectifiers. He did well to hold fast to his fear.

He let it be known around town that he was going to Buttstadt to get his mother and bring her back to Langensalza to visit her grandchildren. He knew he was leaving so many hostages behind that he would hear no objections from the authorities. With his Communist-issued identification intact, Gerhard took the train to Apolda via Erfurt.

Travel by train was much improved. The cars were not overloaded and trains once again ran on time. This last point was very important. He was betting his life and the lives of his family on the German ability to be punctual, occupation or no occupation. At Erfurt he changed trains and during the hour layover he memorized the train schedules posted, arrivals and departures.

From Apolda he walked to Buttstadt. He hadn't been in the town for five minutes before he knew that things were no better in Buttstadt than they were back in Langensalza. There was that East German Look, and nobody wanted to greet him or talk to him about anything more offensive than the fact that the sun was shining.

When he greeted his mother he saw the same look in her eyes, and he was glad that he'd come. She embraced him warmly.

"Gerhard, how good to see you, come in quickly." The last phrase was typical East German. "Get out of sight before somebody sees and reports," was the silent meaning.

He stepped into the house. It was the house of his uncle, Herr Hohlbein, "It is all right, Mama. I have the necessary papers and I'm going to take you to visit the children."

"How wonderful, how are they?"

They talked of family and of children. Gerhard met some of his mother's relatives whom he hadn't seen for years and didn't really remember. He sat down that evening to a very skimpy meal. One ate better when one owned a bakery. The list of topics avoided was endless. Politics were not mentioned. The Occupation was not mentioned; in fact nothing of substance was discussed at all and the evening dragged by, slowly.

* * *

Gerhard and his mother walked to Apolda. Transportation was available, but he wanted to know how well her knee was doing. Also, he wanted to talk. Two people walking down a dirt road can have a conversation without being overheard.

Once clear of Buttstadt his mother laughed. It was the first genuine laugh he had heard in months and he realized how things had changed and how he was changing. The Communists were having their way with him in spite of himself. It was indeed time to leave.

"Why are you laughing?"

"It is like old times. We are walking together again. You better let me have my own suitcase. I have a suspicion that I'm headed for another long walk."

Gerhard, who had been carrying both bags handed her the smaller one. "Take mine, it is lighter than yours. You may have guessed right, but it is better if there are no details. I trust you, Mama, but people slip and say things they cannot draw back. I will tell you what you need to know when you need to know it. Meantime, you are headed for Bad Langensalza to see your grandchildren, and this is true."

"As you wish. I've thought a lot about the last

walk we had. It is strange the way the memory works. I know we had fearful times, and very uncomfortable times, and we were hungry, but still the pleasant parts remain more clearly. We have a way of remembering what it is that we really want to remember." She changed the subject.

"How is Gertrud? How is she taking the Occupation?"

"Like everyone else, she is filled with fear. It keeps her too thin." They walked along chatting about the things they would have chatted about the evening before, at dinner, but couldn't because there had been too many people present. The fact that they were all related to one another was not the protection that it once had been.

It was a beautiful autumn day. The field on their right had been harvested and lay fallow. The farmer had had a stand of corn in it, about a hundred yards long and twenty yards wide. It too had been harvested and the stalks that had been green and straight were now brown, broken and intertwined, leaning one against another. The beauty of this was lost on Gerhard. He pointed at it and spoke with bitterness.

"Germany after the war."

His mother said nothing in return, but his remark had changed their mood and they finished their walk to Apolda in silence.

* * *

The week at Langensalza went quickly. There was little happiness expressed—it would not do to show the occupying power that life was a pleasure. Everyone was tight-lipped and restrained in their conversation, particularly in front of the children. Gerhard had warned his mother about this, unnecessarily. She had become aware of the problem back at Buttstadt, where a child's innocent remark led to the death of a parent.

At the end of a week, Gerhard asked for permission to take his mother back to her home and to have his wife Gertrud accompany him. From Buttstadt, he and Gertrud would go on to Berlin. They would be back in a couple of weeks and they would leave their three children with the grandparents. Permission was granted and Gerhard bought three tickets to Apolda via Erfurt.

Erfurt was as far east as they went. They got off the train there as if to wait for the next one. In the station, Gerhard spoke to Gertrud.

"I want you to look around carefully. You must be very familiar with this station. Go into the lavatory and look around there. Also, look at the tracks and the pedestrian walks between them. You are going to get off one train, go in the station and get back on the wrong train, you and the children. Try to think through each move, and of anything that might occur."

Gertrud looked around. "I understand. Give me a few minutes."

When she was through studying the situation, she came back to her husband and her mother-in-law and nodded. "All right."

Gerhard nodded in return and opened his big suitcase. Out of it he pulled a knapsack. "We are going to have a picnic on the bank of the river. Take your coats and put anything in the pockets that you might need on a long hike."

They did as they were told, and then Gerhard took their three suitcases over to the baggage master and checked them through to Apolda. Passengers with large suitcases going east were not questioned, but people headed west with large suitcases looked suspicious. With his knapsack on his back and a stick in his hand, Gerhard looked for all the world like a man out for a stroll with his wife and mother.

In the bottom of the knapsack he had carefully sewn a notebook with about one-hundred and twenty pages in it. The notebook was the careful elaboration of the original four sheets of paper. With the help of Kostka and Kostka's secretary, he had taken the basic ideas of his inventions and drawn them again and had typed descriptions that showed great detail. With the notebook there was a small sum of money, all he had been able to save from the sale of the rectifiers. The only other things of negotiable value were three gold coins that he had saved since his confirmation. They were well hidden. In order to get to his valuables, it would be necessary to cut the stitching that held the false bottom in place. On top of the false bottom there was food, the kind one would take on a picnic, particularly if one worked in a bakery. The food was covered by his folded coat. They walked out of the station and toward the river. On its bank, they sat and watched the water flow by for a few minutes until Gerhard was sure they hadn't been followed. Then he spoke.

"We are going to take a train to Treffurt, walk across the border to Wanfried and take a train to Frankfurt. All of this will be dangerous, but the most dangerous part is going to be our walk across the border. It is mostly rough terrain, and where it isn't, it is heavily patroled. We'll have to be careful with our strength and food. We may be able to buy something to eat, but again, we may not. If we are questioned, try to let me do the talking. I have the map of the area thoroughly memorized and I have a compass. Whether riding the train or walking I shall always know where we are. When we are walking, if we are stopped, I will give you quietly, the names of two towns. The first will be the town we supposedly left and the second will be the town we're headed for. If you are asked directly you can answer, but try to leave the talking to me."

Anna Dirks laughed. "I know how this works. I've seen it."

"You saw a little, Mama, but this is different. We may be stopped by Russians, not Americans, or worse, we may be stopped by German Communist Police. The border is being more carefully guarded all the time, but one way or another, we shall get to Frankfurt."

A look of terror came across Gertrud's face. "My children."

Gerhard patted his wife's knee. "We shall go back for them, I promise. It is for them we are doing this. Mama will stay in Frankfurt and some day soon all five of us will join her there. You will see."

* * *

In 1947 the Communists were not as thorough nor as clever at caging people in as they became later. After the Berlin wall was built, a wall that was placed like a dam in the face of people fleeing to freedom, the rest of the border tightened up too. But in 1947, when Gerhard got through, any clever man with a map of the area in his head and a compass in his hand, had a decent chance to make it to freedom. Four days after they left Erfurt, they rode into Frankfurt on a train from Fulda.

The difference between East and West was almost overwhelming. In Frankfurt, people were walking around talking to each other in complete freedom. There was an air of hustle and bustle. Much of the populace still looked gaunt and drawn, but the hidden terror was not in their eyes. Frankfurt was where Gerhard wanted to be and he knew it.

"Let us go look at our new 'residence,' " Gerhard suggested and led the way to the Torpedo factory. The building was standing intact and it was divided into sections. In each section some form of manufacturing was taking place. West Germany was back in business. As yet, only in a limited way, but back in business. Some of the buildings around the factory showed signs of damage, but the factory had not been hurt.

"Our problem is this," Gerhard explained, "We need a friend, a relative, or someone we can bribe who will share room with us and with our children until we can find a place of our own. We might have to live with someone for months. Perhaps it won't take that long, but it could happen. We have to find that person. The closer we are to the factory, the better. I may be working there, so we will start with apartment houses in this area and work our way out in concentric circles."

It was Anna Dirks who solved the problem—in only an hour. She found Frau Bill at Winterstasse 16, next to the Torpedo factory. Anna found, when she rang Frau Bill's door bell and began to talk to her, that the elderly lady was on her way to the office of housing, as required by law, to report the fact that she was in her apartment alone. Her husband had just died, and according to the rigid laws governing housing in Frankfurt at that time, she could live there alone no longer.

Frau Dirks was a widow too, and they started talking. It wasn't long until they were seated inside the apartment and reached an agreement. Anna found Gerhard and Gertrud, and they had arranged to meet on the corner every two hours to see if anyone had found anything. Anna met them and took them back to introduce them to Frau Bill. It was soon arranged that the three of them would use the apartment while they were in town, and that Anna Dirks would stay there when Gertrud and Gerhard returned east. Later, after rapport had built up, it was agreed that when Gerhard and

Gertrud returned to Frankfurt with their family, they would all live in the apartment. They would be crowded, but everyone in Frankfurt was crowded. There was an advantage to Frau Bill. If the housing authority looked into her situation, she would be able to show that seven people were living in her apartment. Without this arrangement, she might find strangers moved in with her whether she liked them or not.

Gerhard was able to put frosting on the cake. The widow had neither money nor food. Gerhard had little enough, but he agreed to share whatever they had and whatever they got. The decisions out of the way, the three ladies began to chat happily about other things. Gerhard excused himself, and promising to return soon, headed for the bank that Frau Bill had recommended. It was the one her husband had used.

At the bank, and in front of the notary, Gerhard took his pocket knife out of his pocket, opened it and with the blade cut the stitching and released the false bottom. From under it, he pulled out his note book and his money.

He handed the designs to the notary. "Please look at these carefully. I will sign my name on the back of several of the sheets, and then you will please notarize my signature and the date." It was October 10, 1947.

This was promptly done, Gerhard paid him and walked across the bank lobby to see one of the bank officers. He opened an account and deposited his small amount of cash. The banks of Frankfurt were not the world's most stable, but compared with any other place in Germany, they were safe.

He could not rent a safety deposit box; none was available. The bank had a service, however, and would hold his papers in their main vault until a box became available. He attached a page of instructions to his designs, left the note book with the bank officer and returned to Frau Bill's apartment.

Gerhard was a man in a hurry and the next morning, after expressing gratitude, he and Gertrud bid the two ladies good bye and walked to the train station to catch the next train to Berlin. He left the two widows with a little money and the remainder of the food. Gerhard and his wife would stay hungry until they got back to their apartment in Berlin. They had been hungry before and would be again. Being hungry was part of living in Occupied Europe.

* * *

The train ride from Frankfurt to Berlin was fast and fairly comfortable. Communications and transportation in the West were improving rapidly. They arrived in Berlin in the early evening and had a meal with Kostka. It wasn't much but it was far better than nothing. Then they spent the night at their apartment. The next morning they went to see Huth.

Huth was stunned. "You've been to Frankfurt and you left?"

"Our children are still in Bad Langensalza. We came back for them."

The four of them were sitting in Huth's office: the Dirks, and Huth and Becker. It was Becker who had the next question.

"What did you do with your designs?"

"I left them in trust with a bank in Frankfurt with instructions that if I'm not back within three months, the papers are to be destroyed."

Becker blanched. "You don't trust us? We are taking a risk for you."

"I appreciate this, believe me I do." Gerhard made it sound very sincere; he had no proof of anything out of line, just suspicions. "But there are people above you and below you in your organization who have some idea of what is going on. If someone pointed me out as a man trying to escape to the West and I disappeared into Russia, and my designs disappeared into Remington Rand, who would weep?"

Huth spoke wryly. "Gerhard, I do believe you'll make it to Frankfurt. You seem to think of everything. I have papers ready for you."

Gerhard shook his head. "I don't want to be in Langensalza with papers on me that give me permission to move from Berlin to Frankfurt. You keep all the papers except the permission to ship materials to Berlin. I will be back in Berlin in about a week for the other permits."

SAN FRANCISCO, CALIFORNIA. Gerhard Dirks has just returned from a trip to Germany. Against the advice of friends, he managed to make it into East Germany and out again, without being detained. His brief return sparks many memories, and Dirks does not hesitate to discuss his observations.

"The Russians, at the close of World War II, would have liked to just keep working their way to the Atlantic. They may yet if we are not careful. Several things, though, were responsible for stemming the Communist tide at the end of the war—the stiffening of American policy toward Russia, American power because you had the bomb, and the Marshall Plan. The Marshall Plan, from the German point of view, was the most important reason. Not just the money—that was helpful, but it was the attitude of the United States after the war that was so important. You had beaten us, you could have done the same thing to us that the Russians were doing—strip us naked. Instead, you said 'stand up, get well, and we will help you.' The contrast between the United States and Communist Russia was so great that those of my generation who saw both sides are uncompromisingly anti-communistic. Here was the United States helping, while Russian Communists were tearing up everything that wasn't nailed down, and some things that were, and sending it all back to Russia.

"When I went back to East Germany, I found things only a little better. I returned to Bad Langensalza, to Sommerd, to Leipzig, to the places from which I have escaped. The people, the common people who are not politically connected, do not eat very well, their clothes are old and they live in run down and unpainted houses. Worse, there is the constant *spying and supervision. They are watched constantly. There is no privacy, there is no freedom of movement. They are herded about like sheep. In that sense, nothing has changed.*

"For those who have gone along with the Communists or have become Communists, things are better. They are not as well off as they would be in the West, not by a lot, but they are comparatively well off. Then there are the few who have made themselves very useful to the Russians and they are well off indeed. And it is true, some East Germans are dedicated Communists. You will see quite a show, I think, put on by East Germany in the Olympics in Moscow. There will be swarms of apparently contented people. When you see that, keep one thing in mind—the Wall. It costs the Russians and the East Germans millions of dollars every year, money that they would be glad to spend on something else if they could. That huge, elaborate, cruel wall is there because it has to be. If it were not there, the Germans would pour through to the West like water going through a break in a dam. So when you see big pagentry and thousands of people waving flags, many are there only because the wall is there. The East Germans have a hatred for their government that you can feel.

"Thousands of Russian troops stay in the country to maintain the Communist power in East Germany. We were driving a car, and we went through the mountains and the forests, and whenever we were in areas where the Russians could be at least partly hidden, we saw them, again and again.

"We saw signs, too, big billboard signs in German: 'Russia wants peace, the United States wants the neutron bomb.' These signs are all around. They are afraid of the cruise missile and the neutron bomb. The Russian troops are grouped by the thousands in clusters. One cruise missile and one neutron bomb would wipe out a huge force. If the United States develops these new weapon systems, the Russian military presence is neutralized, and they know this.

"Also, from their point of view, just as bad is the fact that if the cruise missile and the neutron bomb are developed, the Russians will have to disperse their troops. They will have to spread them thin. If they do that, the troops and the tanks can be seen and be counted. Then everyone will know the terrible expenditure in weapons and men necessary for the Russians to have, to keep the East Germans within their power.

"Those whom we talked to in the Western countries who are not allied with the Communist parties are hoping so very much that the United States will go ahead with this weapons system. If they do not, someday the huge Russian forces will cross the border and head for the sea. Without the United States weapons system, there will be nothing to stop them.

"The Communists have another weapon against us—they use American television and West German television for their own purposes. They use our news broadcasts with Russian subtitles, or a Russian translation. Our broadcasts show violence, crime, tension and dishonesty in government, in our free society. They had one television special done by an American *television network on how to protect your house. It showed burglar alarms, window locks, door locks, fences and elaborate lighting systems. When the American program was over, an East German voice said something like, 'In America, people lock themselves in their own jails because the people who should be in jail are free to roam the streets. Do you want freedom like that?'*

"It is a very difficult question to answer, and it is effective propaganda, particularly with the young who have no memory of Communist violence. There, the terrible violence and brutality is carefully hidden from view. We advertize our violence in America, on television and in the newspapers. They make us look bad."

NINE

In Langensalza there were tears and remonstra-
tions. The grandparents were very upset. If Gerhard moved to Frankfurt they would not only miss
him, but they probably would never see their
daughter again, or the children. Those three
beautiful children. How could they say good bye to
them?

In the end Gerhard prevailed. It was in the best
interests of the children that the family move. He
and Gertrud sang the praises of Frankfurt and the
West, the children would be safe, and could grow
up out from under the Communists.

They had called the family council and had met
in the back of the bakery. Lights on in that kitchen
at any hour did not seem out of place, and they had
all reached the building discreetly. The discussion
went as Gerhard had planned until the end, then he
got a surprise. It came from Gertrud's niece.

"Uncle Gerhard, I am coming too." She spoke
very quietly and very firmly. Gerhard sensed a
coming struggle. He did not want to complicate
their escape.

"I cannot take you. Your name is not Dirks,

and I cannot get you false papers. If I could, I would be endangering all the rest of us, do you want that?"

"No. No false papers. I will go as myself, and I will take my chances."

Gerhard studied her. "The NKVD man, he is interested in you?"

"Not the original one, he was transferred. The one who took his place is worse. I have heard stories from some women who have visited him. Uncle Gerhard, I'm going with you. When my invitation comes from him, or someone like him, I don't intend to be here to receive it. Now I go with you and Aunt Gertrud or I go alone."

As Gerhard studied her face he saw the courage in it. She might be an asset as well as a danger. "All right, you can come. I cannot get you a transfer to Frankfurt, but I can and will get you a train ticket. When you leave here for Buttstadt, you are going with Gertrud to help with the children because I am in Berlin. When you get on the train for Frankfurt, you will have only a ticket."

"There is one more thing," here Gerhard began to sound like a fuhrmann, as there was a hard quality to his voice. "All tears will be shed now. When Gertrud leaves here, it is ostensibly to visit my mother. Long drawn out goodbyes and obvious tears will give away the fact that not all is as it is supposed to be. Is that understood?"

Hermann spoke in a quiet, resigned way. "Of course, Gerhard."

* * *

When Gerhard went to the local Communist headquarters for permission to move "materials" to Berlin, he had a permit to do so that was signed by the proper authorities—not low level functionaries, but high level people, British, American and above all, Russian. The local Communist in Langensalza was particularly impressed by the member of the party who had put approval on Gerhard's request. He hadn't known Gerhard had such connections.

"These materials are what, Herr Dirks?"

"They are electronic subassemblies. They are needed for some communication work in Berlin. Also, some other things that friends in Berlin have requested."

The question had been asked out of curiosity rather than any other reason. The signatures on Gerhard's permit made any lack of cooperation out of the question. Huth had done well. The functionaire promptly signed papers giving Gerhard a freight car and access to the local freight yards. Gerhard thanked him and left.

Rather than use the bakery truck, which was busy enough, Gerhard got a horse and wagon from a local drayman and loaded the wagon with what he wanted to take to Frankfurt. This included their furniture, what little they had. It was a pathetic amount when compared with the furnishings that had been theirs in their place in Roztoky. But, pathetic or not, it was needed. The apartment in Frankfurt was bare. Frau Bill had sold some of her furniture to buy food.

Personal things that Dirks wanted were packed first and put in the bottom of the wooden boxes. Over these personal things, electronic parts obtained from the war surplus yard were cleverly spread. They were the ostensible reason for shipping but were probably unnecessary. Gerhard doubted that anyone was going to look at anything. His papers were more than in order, they were authoritative, but he would take every reasonable precaution.

Once the wagon was loaded, Gerhard drove it out to the rail yard and looked for the conductor of the next eastbound train. The man was thoroughly German and was an unhappy as everyone else about the occupation, but Gerhard had no way of conveying to the man that they were of the same mind. When the conductor looked at Gerhard's papers he turned sullen, but remained cooperative. He pointed to three cars sitting on a siding.

"Use any one of those you wish, they are going on the next train to Erfurt. You will have to have your car switched to a Berlin train when you get there. There is no train that goes directly from Langensalza to Berlin."

Two of the three freight cars were partly loaded, the third car was empty. Trains going to Russia were still very heavily loaded with "confiscated" materials, but trains going to Berlin were not too heavily loaded, nor did they run as frequently. Gerhard loaded his things on the empty car.

Deep inside the furniture, and hidden in the other packing cases was the most precious part of the cargo. He had hidden potatoes, almost three hundred pounds of them. They were not quite worth their weight in gold in Frankfurt, but almost. They would not only feed his family, but some of them could be exchanged at a good rate for other foods. Once the freight car was loaded, Gerhard never left it. That meant that he had to stay with the car for twenty-four hours before it moved.

His family did not see him depart. He had said his goodbyes back at the bakery. He would not see them again until the trains crossed in Erfurt, and if one of the trains were late he might never see them again, period.

His ride to Erfurt in the freight car was not too uncomfortable. It was a fairly warm day for the middle of the fall season, and he was able to put himself in a corner between two pieces of furniture and wrap himself in a blanket he had brought. But in Erfurt he ran into his first problem. The train for Berlin was made up and was ready to leave as soon as the engine hooked on. The next freight to Berlin would not be for two more weeks.

The station master was no help. "If you can talk the engineer into it, he can add your car to his train."

Gerhard raced across the tracks from the freight office to the engine getting ready to switch tracks and head up the Berlin bound freight. As he ran he thought about the best approach. Should he try to bribe? Should he cajole? Or should he try fear? The Russian Occupation had so changed society that he knew intuitively that fear was his best weapon.

The engineer looked harried, frustrated, tired, and had the grime on his face that is inevitable for those who work around coal. Gerhard talked to him as one would talk to a stray dog.

"I have a freight car that just came in from Langensalza that must get to Berlin on your train."

"I'm sorry, sir, we're leaving. We pull out," he looked at his watch, "in three and a half minutes."

"I am Herr Doktor Gerhard H. Dirks, and these are my papers. This train is not leaving in three and a half minutes, it is not leaving with you on it at all unless that freight car is added to this train." He pointed at the car containing his things.

The engineer looked at the papers. They were very impressive. He was trapped. He could call the local authority in Erfurt, but supposing there was tension between the authority in Erfurt and the authority in Berlin? He could open a Pandora's box. Or, he could throw the man off his engine, but there were engineers who had been with the railway for years who had disappeared without leaving a trace. Maybe this was why they disappeared, they had crossed someone like Dirks, whoever he was.

He looked at his watch again. If he did not leave on time, the station master would be a little unhappy. The scheduling between Erfurt and Berlin might have to be re-timed. If he "hooked up" and left with his train intact, this stranger would be furious. The engineer decided to take his chances with the station master. He knew him. Dirks was a mystery.

"All right, Herr Doktor Dirks, we will do it as fast as we can."

Gerhard almost said, thank you, but realized in time that this would not fit in too well with his pose as an autocrat, so instead he said, "Yes, indeed you will."

* * *

The situation in the freight yard at Berlin was worse than it had been in Erfurt, worse by far. The confusion was greater, the traffic heavier and the delay longer. This time, when Gerhard confronted the station master he had no authority with which he could bluff. Berlin was not Erfurt—he couldn't throw his weight around. Also, Berlin was as far as his Russian authority extended. All Gerhard could show the station master was the transfer moving him, his family and his possessions from Berlin to Frankfurt. Such papers were common; the station master saw a dozen such transfers in a day, from Berlin to many other cities. He told Gerhard to put "Gerhard Dirks" on the list, and beside the name write the destination and the number of his freight car. In three months, the car would be attached to a train going to Frankfurt. In three months, three hundred pounds of priceless potatoes would be rotten.

Gerhard did as he was told and put his name on the list. He was on the fourteenth page. He looked at the names on the first page, those who would be whipping things on trains in the near future. He saw a name he recognized, Bauer. Bauer was a common name, but the first name was the same and it would be the banker who had been on the garbage detail with Gerhard, the man who had had the bad back and did only the driving. Gerhard copied off the full name and the number of the freight car assigned to Bauer. It too was going to Frankfurt. He went looking for Bauer, hoping the man was still a banker. It would make him easier to find.

Once again Huth helped. He took the name from Gerhard and called his own banker. No, the banker didn't know Herr Bauer, but if Bauer was in the banking business in Berlin, he could be found. It took less than an hour. While Gerhard waited, Huth's banker found Bauer and gave Huth the address of the bank where the man was working. Time was of the essence. Gerhard did not know for sure when the train with Bauer's things would be leaving Berlin, maybe in an hour, maybe in a day or a week, no one knew.

Gerhard found Bauer at his desk in a downtown Berlin bank. It was hard to realize that he had known the man as a driver of a garbage truck. Bauer was every inch the German banker. Gerhard felt seedy by comparison. Although he had taken a bath in his Berlin apartment and gotten the dirt from his freight train ride out of his hair, he was not wearing decent looking clothes. He didn't own any and he looked "East German."

Bauer spoke first. "Doktor Dirks, it is good to see you again, sit down." Gerhard took the seat offered and mumbled his thanks. Bauer continued in a warm tone of voice. Apparently the informality was gone but the friendliness was still intact. "You were a help to me. If I had had to bend over, I would not have been able to hold that job, and at that time I needed that job. Enough of the past, what can I do for you now?"

Gerhard explained his situation and showed Bauer the papers transferring him from West Berlin to Frankfurt. "My possessions, such as they are, are sitting in a freight car in the Berlin switching yards. I am told it will be weeks until the car is sent to Frankfurt."

"I'm also being transferred to Frankfurt," the banker admitted, "This is a happy coincidence."

"I know," Gerhard admitted, "I saw your name on the station master's list in the freight yard. Your things are to be shipped soon."

"This week." There was a moment's silence and then the banker asked again, "What do you want me to do?"

Gerhard pulled the manifest of his own shipment out of his pocket. "Please let me include my things as though they were part of yours so they will go soon also. When I get to Frankfurt I shall need those things desperately." He didn't add that without them, his family might starve, if his family ever got to Frankfurt. "Add my things to your manifest, and I will carry everything one item at a time from my car to yours."

Bauer shook his head. "I can't. Shipping is terribly tight. They have allotted me space for only what I need."

Gerhard's heart sank. "Can you think of any way?"

"There is a man with power to do it and he is shipping things to Frankfurt too. Do you happen to know Dr. Kinne?"

Gerhard's relief was immediate and obvious. "We are good friends, he has helped me in the past."

Bauer reached for the phone on his desk, "Let me see if I can get him on the phone for you."

The connection was promptly made and Gerhard found himself talking to his friend and mentor, explaining his problem. With Dr. Kinne, it was no problem. He took the freight car number from Gerhard and said he would send a letter with it allowing Gerhard Dirks to enter "his" car. The car would be in the freight yards in Frankfurt in less than a week. Gerhard was profuse in his thanks and hung up the phone.

He turned to Bauer. "Thank you for your help, now I have a question. Is there danger of losing things; should I ride the car?"

"No, my friend. Between West Berlin and Frankfurt, it is like old times. Your things will be safe, I'm sure of it. I have no worry for my own shipment."

"Thank you again." Gerhard got up to go.

"You are more than welcome, and still we are not even. If I can do more for you, I will be in Frankfurt in a month or two. Here is my new business card. Come to the bank and see me."

Gerhard looked at the card. It gave the name and address of the bank where he had left his drawings and made his deposit. He almost said, "I'm already a customer," but he checked himself in time. His years in Communist territory had taught him—never give anyone any unnecessary information. Bauer might not want to know that Gerhard had already been to Frankfurt.

TEN

After two long weeks of waiting, Gerhard went to the passenger train station, his transfer to Frankfurt in hand, and bought six tickets to Frankfurt. The train would leave early the next morning. Gerhard was at the station an hour before departure time. He wanted to watch the gateman punching the tickets of the passengers on their way to the train. Gerhard was going to be only one person, and he was going to have six tickets.

He watched and waited. The policeman standing next to the gateman stepped away. Gerhard worked his way into the line quickly. At the gate he handed over six tickets and looked the man straight in the eye.

"My family will be here shortly. I'll stand inside and wait for them."

The gateman knew he was lying, but Germans were helping each other. He nodded and punched six tickets. Gerhard stepped through the gate and stood there long enough to make it look good, and then made his way to the train.

The next hurdle was going to be the conductor

and the police who would be accompanying him. On the west bound train the punched tickets were examined and marked. The usual procedure was for a couple of military police to ride from Berlin to Wittenburg and walk through the passenger cars with the conductor. They would examine everyone's papers and watch the tickets being marked. At Wittenburg the train would come to a stop long enough to let them off, and then continue on its way to Frankfurt, via Erfurt. At Erfurt, the crews would be changed and a Volkpolizei, an East German policeman, would get on the train with the new crew and look again at everyone's papers. At the border of West Germany, the train would stop again and let off the policeman and anyone he'd caught trying to get to the West without proper authority. Gerhard's problem was to get the Berlin conductor to mark six tickets leaving Berlin when there was only one passenger.

Half way to Wittenburg, with the train still moving at half speed, the conductor and the military personnel entered the car. Gerhard had boarded at the last possible moment. By getting on last, he could look the car over and pick a seat where no one would be sitting right beside him. So far, so good. Then he got a real break. The two people across the aisle from him had tickets and got them marked, but there was something wrong with their papers. The military started asking questions, the conductor waited, looking bored.

Gerhard reached out and pulled gently on the

bottom of the man's uniform coat. The conductor turned around. Gerhard held out six tickets. They looked at each other. There was an almost imperceptable nod from the conductor and the marks were made.

The military, through with the men across the aisle, turned to Dirks. He had carefully separated his travel permit from the other four, and pocketed five of the tickets. They glanced at his permit, at his West Berlin identification and his West Berlin address and walked forward to the next passenger. They had moved quite a way down the car before Gerhard felt safe enough to take his handkerchief out of his pocket and wipe the sweat off his face.

* * *

Gertrud controlled her fear, but not easily. Her hands were cold and clammy and her heartbeat was irregular. She was glad she had her niece; the young girl was like a rock. Hermann had driven them to the station in Langensalza early enough to catch the train for Erfurt. He had not waited to see them off, he did not trust himself not to break down. The children were aware of nothing different, they had merely been told that they were going to Buttstadt to see their grandmother. This was fine with them and they were in a natural and happy mood. Gerhard caught herself snapping at Rainer over nothing and took hold of herself again. She must be careful. The child was seven years old now, and had heard Communist propaganda. He was beginning to be harder to handle. It would be good to get him into the West and with his father.

She looked at the station clock and her heart sank. The train should have been in the station. There was only a ten minute overlay at Erfurt. If they were late?

She heard the train and then saw it. It was only three minutes late. Hopefully that would be made up by the time they reached Erfurt. On board, she picked two pair of empty seats on the left side of the car, facing forward. Gerhard had promised to be standing at the vestibule window of the forward-most car on his Berlin to Frankfurt train. If he had caught his train, he would be standing there and she would see him before she got off her car.

The conductor came through to punch their tickets. He was accompanied by an officious member of the newly formed German Communist home guard. Usually the Russians were careful to look closely at west bound trains, but anyone might be assigned to watch one headed east. Some zealots would watch without being assigned just for the train ride. This young man was immediately smitten with Gertrud's niece. He was full of questions.

She handled him easily, her years in the bakery stood her in good stead. She asked him questions. Did he ever get to Langensalza? Had he ever been in her grandfather's bakery? No? Well she was on her way to Buttstadt to help with the children, but she'd be back in the bakery in a few days. Why didn't he come to the bakery and have a pastry and get acquainted? He lapped it up, asked a few additional questions and went his way through the car accompanying the conductor and preening his imaginary feathers.

By the time the train left Gotha it was still three minutes late and there were only twenty-four kilometers. Gertrud did not share her husband's atheism and she prayed regularly, but never had she prayed more fervently than she did now. "Oh, God have mercy," she prayed over and over.

Finally, her train slid into the Erfurt station. She caught a glimpse of her husband standing against the window as he had promised he would. He saw her but made no sign. The two older children, Rainer and Ingrid, had been told that they were playing a game on their father, and he must be surprised. They were not to see him, not until he saw them. Wolfgang, the youngest and only four, didn't understand and when he saw his father as he looked through the train window he started to call out. Gertrud caught him in time. Her niece distracted the other two so there would be no surreptitious sign of recognition from them. She distracted them a little too much, and Ingrid, now six years old, left her favorite doll on the train when she disembarked.

The five of them, two women and three children, got off the train and went into the station. Gerhard had warned her not to get back on the other train too early. If she got on the Frankfurt train at the last moment, it would not leave time for someone to realize that she had changed trains. She walked into the lavatory and shook for a minute until she had herself back together. She kept repeating her prayer to herself, "God have mercy, God have mercy."

She went back into the main waiting room where the children were standing with their older cousin. She saw the hand on the station clock move and heard the conductor call. Out the door they went, they could hurry, their reason for doing so was obvious, the train was about to leave. At this point Ingrid remembered her doll.

Between them and their train a Volkpolizei was strolling. Before Gertrud could stop the child, she had walked up to the policeman, pointed at the train they had just exited and said, "I left my doll on there. Can you get it for me?"

Gertrud, in spite of her terror, kept her head. She hauled off and slapped Ingrid, hard, right across the face. "That's the wrong train, you stupid child."

Ingrid, who had never before been slapped, never in her life, even for doing wrong, suddenly found herself judged, condemned and punished without due cause and she let out a yell. Gertrud grabbed her by the hand and jerked her toward the Frankfurt train saying to the East German policeman, "This child is going crazy."

The policeman laughed and let her continue on her way. Gerhard had witnessed the scene through the window of the Frankfurt train, and when he saw his wife permitted to continue on her way to him his sense of relief was overwhelming. He leaned his head against the rail car window, closed his eyes and let out a moan. He hadn't realized until then, he'd been holding his breath.

The train left the station immediately and began its journey to the West. Gerhard waited until his heart stopped pounding and then walked back through the passenger cars to where his family had seated themselves. Rainer said nothing to him, as he had been instructed. Ingrid was still crying. Wolfgang saw his father and reached for him. Gerhard picked him up and put him in his lap as he sat down next to his wife. She was shaking uncontrollably. He put a hand on her knee and squeezed.

"It's all right, Gertrud, it's all right."

When she didn't stop shaking, Gerhard left her and went into the next car where he had been sitting and retrieved his suit case from the overhead rack. He took it back to Gertrud, opened it and produced something rarely seen in Germany in 1947, aspirin. The suitcase also contained a canteen. He handed Gertrud two pills and the canteen. She was shaking so badly that he was afraid that if she got the canteen too close to her mouth she'd break her teeth. He took it away.

"Just chew them up and swallow them dry."

She did as she was told, with difficulty. Fifteen minutes went by before the new conductor, accompanied by Volkspolizei, started through the car. Gerhard saw that it was not the same officer that had talked to Gertrud on the station platform and let out another sigh of relief. He pulled his tickets out of his pocket and fanned them like a poker hand. There were six tickets, Berlin to Frankfurt, and all were stamped and punched by the Berlin personnel. The permits, only five, were fanned out behind the tickets in a way that let them overlap slightly. Gerhard hoped that the six tickets, easily counted, would imply six permits, not so easily counted. He didn't want his niece questioned.

It worked. The conductor recognized the marks of the previous conductor and walked on. The East German policeman looked bored. Gerhard guessed that he was suffering the effects of a solid "hangover." He was happy to assume that if there were six tickets there were six passes and that they had already been inspected.

He nodded. Gerhard said, "Guten Tag."

They continued to work their way through the car.

Gertrud had stopped shaking, but Gerhard thought the policeman was so blasé and so physically distressed that he wouldn't have noticed if she hadn't. If the same officer was going to make the final inspection of their train at the border, their chances of all getting through were good.

He wrestled with his conscience for an hour before he spoke to his niece. "I think that the same policeman will come through again; he seems rather careless and I don't think he feels well. It would surprise me if he examined things closely when we get to West Germany. Why don't you just sit here with us?"

She shook her head. "I said I would not endanger all of you by coming, and I won't. We do not know that we will be inspected by the same man, and we do not know, if we get the same man, whether or not he was careless this time, because he will be careful when he gets to the border." she paused. "Can you tell me when we will be at the border?"

He looked at his watch. "In about forty-five minutes."

"In forty minutes, I will go to the toilet and lock myself in."

"All right, but when the train stops, unlock the door. If the door is tried and is locked, it's a dead giveaway, if it is not locked and you stand to one side, you may not be seen even if it is opened."

"Good, thank you. Now, if they find me, I don't know you and never saw you before. You don't know me. I just go on the train at Erfurt and started helping with the children. You address is Berlin, mine is Bad Langensalza. There is no necessary connection. Give me the sixth ticket. I will flush it down the toilet."

In spite of himself, Gerhard felt relieved. "Thank you."

The time passed and she left her seat. The train began to slow down very gradually. They were approaching the border, the border between the Communist East and the West, the border between slavery and freedom. Looking out the window and ahead, Gerhard could see the ugly barbed wire and the guard house that marked the border. The barbed wire was there to "protect" those who lived in the East.

The same guard and the same conductor

walked through the train. They looked at little and Gerhard regretted not insisting that his niece stay with them. Where there had been six, there were now five. That might be quite noticeable. It wasn't. The authorities were looking only for those who added themselves to the train, not for those who left. Despotism was pushing people west, not east. A larger number would be important, a smaller number was of no interest. The guard didn't even try the door of the women's toilet, but walked on through to the next car. In a few minutes, with a West German crew, the train started up again and eased itself through the gap in the fence.

As soon as they had picked up a little speed, Gerhard saw his niece walking toward him. She too was free. He had learned to love her. She was calm, cool and very much in charge of herself. The man who got her for a wife would have himself a prize. She sat down and put her arm around Ingrid. The little girl was quite calm now, but still red-eyed from her weeping. Her mother's slap had hurt in every way. No one had dared explain.

Wolfgang surveyed the three adults from his perch on his father's lap. He looked at them curiously a couple of times, turning from face to face.

"Mama," he asked, "Why is everybody crying?"

She reached over and stroked his face, giving him the answer parents have given since time immemorial, "When you are older, darling, you will understand."

Part II

THE CONVERSION

The first few weeks in Frankfurt were the hardest weeks that Gerhard had ever endured. There was suffering for his family and for him from the first day. Their train had arrived in Frankfurt too late in the evening for them to be able to use the necessary public transportation. Frau Bill's apartment was too far from the station; the children could not possibly have walked the distance, and Gerhard certainly could not afford to hire a taxi. They had to spend the night in the train station.

There were two large rooms on the lower level known as "Bunker Hotel." One room was full of bunks for men and the other for women. They decided to use the facilities. Had they known what was waiting for them, they would have stayed somewhere else if they had had to stand up all night.

The next morning they arrived at Frau Bill's with everybody scratching themselves. It didn't take much of an examination to find lice. Frau Bill knew where the delousing facility was. It was not infrequently used in those days, and they went to it promptly. It was a humiliating experience. The

Dirks' family, together with many other people, stood naked while all the hair on their bodies was cut off and they were scrubbed with a stiff brush covered with yellow soap, and then rinsed off with a hose. Their clothes were thrown into a steam chamber, and kept under pressure for a while. When they got them back, the clothes looked even worse than they had before they were steamed, if that was possible.

There was not only the delousing, there was also near starvation. Gerhard was afraid to spend money even for food until he knew where he would be able to earn some more. The potatoes he had smuggled in literally saved their lives. The children ate the potatoes, one or two a day, and Gerhard and Gertrud and the two old ladies made a "soup" out of the peelings and drank it. Gradually they looked more and more like skeletons.

Gertrud's niece was not able to help. She got a job taking care of small children for a Frankfurt family, but some food, clothing, and a place to sleep was the total wages that came with the job. There was precious little to spare in the home where she worked, and when she did visit the Dirkses she could bring nothing with her.

When Gerhard had just about lost all hope, Doktor Alfred Kinne came to the rescue yet again. The Dirks' address was known to Kinne, and he mailed Gerhard a page cut out of a technical publication that contained an interesting advertisement. It said that the Association of German Machine Manufactures was looking for someone to help them get better organized and to take charge of production control. In his note, Kinne pointed out to his friend that the Skoda experience gave Gerhard good reason to think that the job could be his.

After a family consultation, a few of the precious marks were spent to make Gerhard presentable. A suit, a shirt, a tie and a decent pair of shoes were purchased. Also, he ate a small meal before the interview. The food lessened the haggard look on his face.

The interview went well. His record of previous employment was impressive. Kinne vouched for the truth of it and used what influence he had on Gerhard's behalf. Gerhard got the job. Now there was income, and he was willing to spend what he had in the bank. They bought food, real food, anything but potatoes, and they bought some clothes and looked decent again. Things were soon going very well. Gerhard added to his more than adequate salary by "moonlighting" as a consultant in cost accounting and production control. He worked intermittently for some of Germany's largest firms.

This extra income was set aside for the development of the computer equipment that he had designed on the sands of Wannsee. This too was to be a success. The solid proof lay ahead—he was to sign licensing agreements with Siemag of Germany in October of 1954 and with ICT (then ICL) of Great Britain in April of 1957. In July of the same year he was to sign Zuse of Germany. Farther down the road, Remington Rand and IBM negotiations ended successfully. Also, Bull of France ultimately came around.

In all of this there was to be one unhappy factor. Those who had talked to Gerhard in Berlin had not realized the completeness of Gerhard's notarized design, nor did they know that these drawings and designs would form the basis of a patent, and a series of patents that would stand up in court. The years ahead would hold some lengthy litigation.

These things were in the future. In October of 1953 his days and nights were crammed with product development, with consulting, with committee meetings and with constant negotiations. It was time for a holiday. He and Gertrud could get away together, the children were rapidly growing, and were busy at school.

After studying a map of Switzerland, they decided to visit Lugano. That town and lake are nestled in the Swiss-Italian Alps, one of the most beautiful parts of the world. They drove their new car in a leisurely manner from Frankfurt and, after three days, checked into their hotel in Lugano.

Gerhard, always restless, began to look for some way to amuse himself. Glancing through the window of their hotel room, he could see boats on the lake. That was for him.

"Gertrud, it is a warm day. Let's do some boating."

"I'd rather not, but I'd like to go with you to the shore. I will sit on a bench at the edge of the lake, and you rent a boat for a while." She could not match her husband's energy at work or at play.

At the dock, Gerhard looked at the sail boats but decided against one of them; there was too little wind, and he had had too little experience as a sailor. There were some paddle boats that intrigued him. They were a two pontoon arrangement with a seat between. He rented one and got on it.

Never one to do things by degrees, he paddled straight out into the lake. He was no longer the thin, almost skeletal German who had arrived in Frankfurt. He was now a man of substantial girth, with more weight than the pontoon on the right could sustain. It had a hole in it that was usually above the water line. With Gerhard aboard, that changed. In time Gerhard slowly listed to starboard. He turned and headed back to shore but it was obvious that he was not going to make it. It was not a great matter, the day was warm, he was lightly clothed and a good swimmer. He began to laugh. In a few minutes the pontoon went under and so did Gerhard. He came up spluttering with laughter, he thought it was one of the funniest things that had ever happened to him. The remaining pontoon, still intact, floated the paddle boat, upside down, and kept Gerhard's head above water. Still laughing he began to swim to shore pulling the pontoon behind him.

The day was warm, but the water was not. He was in it for half an hour. It seemed at first to be very invigorating. He made it back to the dock where Gertrud was waiting for him, laughing right along with him. It had been a funny sight. It had seemed as though the boat had quietly "given up" and like the camel with the extra straw, collapsed.

"You are cold, Gerhard?"

He stood on the dock, his clothes dripping water. "Only for a few more minutes. It is a warm day, I shall soon dry out and be comfortable."

It didn't work that way. In a few minutes, he felt even colder. When he told Gertrud, they decided to go up to their hotel and he'd bathe and lie down for a bit. The bath didn't do much good. He was no longer cold, but he still didn't feel well. Gertrud wanted to call a doctor, but he wouldn't hear of it. The next day he would feel fine. The next day he didn't.

He suggested they drive down to the Italian Riviera. They went through Milano and down to the coast to Genova. Here they turned, and drove the shore line, west toward Sanremo. It was a cool, windy and very clear day. They took one spur in the road that took them over high ground. They thought that in the distance they could see the tips of the Corsican mountains.

At Alassio the mountains that divide France from Italy reach the sea. Here they found a hotel that was comfortable and took a room that gave them a view of the Mediterranean.

It was warmer the next day, and warmer than it would have been in Switzerland. Gerhard hoped that by lying around and taking it easy, he'd get his strength back. In a few days he knew it was futile.

"Gertrud, I think we'd better go home. I still

don't feel very well and I'm getting no better."

She could tell that by looking at him, and she was worried. She had never before seen him in a lethargic mood. Worse, the color of his skin was very poor. Something was wrong with his circulation.

"Won't you let me get a doctor?"

"No. I want a German doctor. We will go home."

* * *

Gerhard's doctor entered the Dirks' apartment in Frankfurt and looked around. The furnishings were a symbol of the rise of Western Germany. In eight short years, with the help of the United States, things had changed. Where there had been rubble and despair, there were stately buildings and wealth growing at an ever increasing rate.

The maid had let the doctor in, and now Gertrud came forward to greet him. "Thank you for coming, Doctor. Gerhard is in on his bed; come this way please."

The doctor took one look at Gerhard and saw what he had expected to see. "I'm happy that you are alive and pleased to see that you are in bed. Sit up and let me take your blood pressure and listen to your heart."

With help, Gerhard did as he had been asked and the doctor started listening through his stethoscope. Then he took Gerhard's blood pressure.

When he was through, he folded his arms and

looked down at his patient. He was a successful physician and he had a good bedside manner when he wanted it. He could also be tough.

"My friend, I have been expecting this for some time. You cannot put on weight the way you have been putting it on and stay well. If you did not have the heart of an ox you would already be dead."

"So, what do I do? Do you have some medicine?"

"Yes, and it will make you feel better, so before I give it to you we have to reach an understanding. You are going to have to change your lifestyle. You are going to have to lose weight."

"Doctor, you know better than that. People don't change any more than a machine changes. The computer looks into storage and picks previously placed information, or previously solved questions and combines the old information into another answer. A computer is the sum total of what has been put into it. I am the sum total of my background, what has entered through my senses and the total of all decisions I have made. I am nothing more and I can want to change but I can't do it."

"So, you have been studying cybernetics and now you think there is no difference between a man and a machine."

"You are overstating it, but basically, yes."

"Well, I won't argue with you about it. The way you feel, I don't want to argue with you about anything, not until your blood pressure is down. Machine or no machine, past behavior or no past behavior, you can be put where you can't eat."

"That is different, but I don't want to go there."

"You have a choice, Gerhard," here the doctor spoke more kindly. "You can go to where they will control you and then you will live for a while. Or you can go on like you are doing, and you will be dead in three months, six months, a year at the most. Looking back into your subconscious and pulling out previous decisions, which do you want?"

There was a long silence while Gerhard struggled with himself. He was in the middle of several things that had been set aside for his vacation and he was anxious to get back to them. If he felt better he'd be able to work.

"I'll go away in a month."

The doctor shook his head. "No. Now."

"Where?"

"A clinic at Bad Pyrmont."

"Where is it?"

"It is north of Kassel, but not so far north as to be in the flat land. It is hilly, very pretty country."

"What will they feed me?"

"Nothing." The doctor opened his bag, replaced his stethoscope and took out a bottle of pills. He put half a dozen in a small envelope. "Take one of these pills now, and one more each morning and evening until you get to the clinic. At the clinic, the doctor there will take over your medication. I will phone him in the morning and tell him you are going to be there in forty-eight hours. Until you get there, eat about half of what you have been eating, and stop drinking beer. And no coffee or tea. Water only. If you want to skim the cream off some milk, you can drink a little of the milk."

The doctor knew that after a couple of pills, Gerhard was going to feel better and not be so docile about going to the clinic, so he gave him a parting warning. "If you do not go to the clinic, when you don't feel well again, don't call me. Find another doctor."

At that point Gerhard knew he had no choice. "All right, Doctor, I will go."

* * *

The first three days at the clinic were the worst. They gave him water, a vitamin drink and one teaspoon full of honey. He could think of nothing but his hunger. The medical staff monitored his blood pressure and heart frequently. By the fourth day, things were better. The lethargy left him and he began to read the copy of the poetic works of Goethe which he had brought with him. It had been years since he had read anything, just to read. It was a long-forgotten pleasure, and he read with understanding and retention. He was no longer muddle-headed. His blood pressure had come down and he was thinking clearly. He felt like he could solve any problem he put his mind to.

In the middle of the afternoon of the fourth day, he came to a stopping place in his book, put it down and strolled out into the lobby of the clinic. There was a man standing in the lobby, looking out the window at the gray day. There was a little drizzle falling. He looked familiar but it was a few minutes before Gerhard was able to place him. It was Fritz Waldheim, an engineer with whom Gerhard had worked in the past. He was a brilliant man and a hard driver like Dirks. They had worked well together; they were both tough and tough-minded. Waldheim had joined the Nazi party for the usual reasons. He had wanted to advance his career and do what, at the time, seemed best for the glory of Germany.

When Dirks approached Fritz Waldheim he saw no sign of recognition on the man's face. Then he remembered. Fritz had known him when he had been very thin. They had both put on weight, but Gerhard had put on far more.

"Herr Waldheim?"

He looked at Gerhard and raised his eyebrows. "Yes?"

"You do not recognize me. I'm too fat."

Fritz smiled. "Now that you speak, I do. Gerhard Dirks, how are you?" He extended his hand and Gerhard shook it as he answered.

"I'm fine, except I weigh too much. That's why they have me here. Are you here for the same reason?"

Fritz put his hands on his stomach. "I'm afraid so." He pointed to a couple of chairs in the corner of the lobby. "Let's sit there and talk for a bit." They seated themselves and Waldheim continued. "I see your name from time to time in connection with the manufacturer's association. You must be doing well with them. What else are you doing? I do not remember you as a man who would be satisfied with only one job."

Gerhard smiled. He was pleased by the compliment and he began to talk about his computer work, about his family and about his escape from the East. Fritz kept him going with an occasional question. After an hour something dawned on Gerhard. Fritz had said nothing about himself. That was not like the Fritz that Gerhard remembered. There was something about the man that seemed different.

"The first days here have been very restful," Gerhard mentioned, "but I wonder if I shall not be bored soon. The doctor wouldn't let me bring work with me. I've been reading Goethe, but one can get enough even of Goethe after two or three weeks. What do you do with your time?"

"I'm reading too, but I have been fortunate. I've been meeting here in Bad Pyrmont with some friends."

"Electrical engineers?"

"No, I'm the only one of those."

"Politics?" Waldheim shook his head. "Not religion?"

"Yes, I'm a Christian now. I have put my faith in Christ and he has changed my life. I'm meeting with a group of men, some of whom have had the same experience and some of whom are inquiring about it. We meet for prayer, for Bible study and for discussion. All this has made my life completely different."

Gerhard clamped his jaw for a moment and then spoke. "Nobody, but nobody changes."

Waldheim studied him. That last remark had been too dogmatic, there was something going on in Dirks, whether he knew it or not. "You are right, Gerhard, in one sense. I'm still the same, we are all the product of what we have been. But something new has been added." He decided to talk Gerhard's language. "When a computer comes up with an answer, it has polled what has been previously put in it, and ingested the new data. Man's mind works the same way, but when the Spirit of Christ enters a man's mind, there is a new decision force, something that makes us uncomfortable if we make the decision which is only the product of what has gone before. You are right, I have not changed, but yet I have changed, for there is something in me that was not there before. Now I have freedom, I can choose between what is the product of my mechanism, and what is the will of Christ. Until He came into me, there was no freedom. I was just like you."

Gerhard was trapped by his opening remark. He had admitted he had no freedom to change. He didn't know what to say. If he said, as he had said to others, "I'm an atheist" it would sound a little hollow in Waldheim's presence and he couldn't figure out why. Gerhard was a lawyer by training if not by profession and he knew the old principle. "Get a man to talk about himself and he'll repeat himself and there will be contradictions." He asked Fritz to talk about his experience.

From Gerhard's point of view, it didn't work out well at all. Fritz talked for an hour and it became obvious that he was not making up a story, he was just talking about what had happened in him and to him. He confirmed Gerhard's worst fears. The man had changed. The driving self-interest was gone. There was patience and there was an inner peace. When they parted company, Gerhard agreed to attend the week's conference and listen to a man named Richter make several talks.

After they had separated, Gerhard wondered why he had agreed to go. He had no real interest. After he considered the matter for a while, he decided that the change in Fritz had influenced him. There was peace—peace with the world around him and peace with himself. This appealed to the restless, self-driving Gerhard, far more than he wanted to admit. He was not familiar with Augustine's remark, "Thou hast made us for Thyself and our souls are restless until they find their rest in Thee." He had never read the statement but he was experiencing it nonetheless. Gerhard was restless and he knew it. Fritz was no longer restless and his calmness and inner peace were both irritating and, at the same time, appealing.

Gerhard went back to his room and sat at his desk. The pleasure he had experienced as he read Goethe didn't return when he opened the book again. The beauty of it was gone and it was dry and hard to read. He closed the book and looked around for something else. Nothing he saw interested him, and then a thought crossed his mind.

"When all else fails, turn to the source."

He started looking for a Bible. There was none in his room, so he went to the lobby. He approached the attendant at the desk, intending to ask the young man for one. He stopped himself, he didn't want to admit he would be reading it. That gave him pause. Why would he not want anyone to know? He heard himself ask the attendant for the location of a book store. There was one a half dozen streets away. Out the door he went and he walked briskly in the direction that had been indicated.

The book store was a very large one; there were books on all sides placed on shelves that were built to the ceiling, and there were ladders against the walls that made the upper shelves accessible. An older man wearing thick glasses approached Gerhard. He asked if he could help.

"Do you sell Bibles?" Gerhard asked.

"Yes, sir. This way." The man took his place on the far side of the counter. "What kind of a Bible were you interested in, sir?"

"German, of course."

"There are several translations into German. Do you want a Catholic Bible or a Protestant one? Do you want Old German, or something more modern? Do you want a large Bible for decoration, or do you want a small size that you can hold in your hand?"

"I'm going to read it," Gerhard admitted, "And I'll take a Protestant one in modern German."

He was handed a Bible slightly larger than pocket size. "This one I recommend, sir. The German is good and it is quite readable."

Gerhard took it without opening it, paid for it, and left the store.

Back at his room he sat down at his desk and began reading the New Testament. At first the modern German bothered him. He was used to the style of the old German text he'd used as a child. But he was also honest enough to admit to himself why the new German upset him a little. He wanted the old, sonorus, stilted text because that text didn't sound so believable. The modern German brought the things he was reading right up to date, and that was disquieting.

The story itself was disquieting. He read slowly and carefully and he read all four Gospels. He had read them as a child, but now he read them as an adult. The story wasn't like he'd remembered it at all. His memory had said that it was a very beautiful story. Now, as he read it, the story didn't seem beautiful, it was filled with "angst," dread. Either the man Jesus was crazy, or he was the Son of God, or more likely, the story was just fiction.

He chose the third explanation and pushed down the logical question that followed his choice. Why would anyone make up a story like that? He could make up a better one himself, one in which the good triumphed and you wouldn't have to pretend that a loser had risen from the dead.

He didn't want to go to the meeting that night anyway, and the reading had only made his desire to stay away grow stronger. He looked down at his hands. "Angstachweiss," cold sweat, covered them.

He brought his fist down on the desk. This was nonsense. He'd go to that meeting, listen to those super-religious people and put his own disquieting feelings away where they belonged.

* * *

Richter's talk was on the contrast between Pietism and social action. Gerhard was not particularly interested. He was studying the group. The men had little in common, outwardly. They seemed to be from all walks of life and from differing educational backgrounds. What had brought them together? He wasn't sure that Richter's talk was really the center of things, he had the feeling that these men just wanted to be in each other's company.

It was the question and answer period following the talk that really bothered Gerhard. He'd been in many such situations in business and in school, and he was used to the "attack-defense" stance between speaker and audience. In such situations, each person pushed a particular point of view in order to call attention to himself. At this meeting there was none of that. Those who talked seemed to want information, or to bring up a point that should be considered. No one tried to show off or to argue just to argue. The same calm attitude that characterized Fritz and Richter seemed to characterize those in the group who contributed or answered questions.

When the meeting was over, the men stood around and drank coffee. Fritz introduced Gerhard to several of them. It bothered Gerhard no end that everyone was perfectly at ease except him. He was used to making people feel uncomfortable around him, particularly people who were incompetents. Now the shoe was on the other foot and he didn't like it.

The worst moment came when one of the men he had just met asked him if he was a Christian.

"Of course I'm a Christian," Gerhard answered, "I was confirmed and baptized into the German Lutheran Church." The men in the small group around him chuckled. "What are you laughing at?" He was really upset.

Fritz gave him a soothing answer. "Most of us have been through that. I'm afraid it doesn't mean anything. It can mean something of course. For some people it is the difference between spiritual life and death, but that is when they make a conscious choice, not when they follow a social custom because their parents made them. God takes us into Christ one at a time. We have to participate in our own conversion."

Gerhard didn't know what to say, so he stood there and listened to the conversation for a few more minutes and then after promising to return to the meeting the following night, he made his excuses and left.

* * *

When Gerhard saw Fritz at the clinic the next

day, he was prepared to attack. The argument that "people can't change" was getting hard to defend; he'd bring out his big gun, data storage. They were sitting in the lobby where they had sat the day before and chatted for a few minutes. Fritz brought the conversation around to serious things with a question.

"How did you like last night's meeting?"

"Fine." That wasn't exactly true, but it would do for an answer. "I have a question for you."

"Go ahead and ask." Fritz pulled out his pipe and began to prepare it for lighting. Living at the clinic on a starvation diet had turned his pipe into a blessing.

"Do you believe in a final day of judgment, like we were taught to believe in our Lutheran catachism classes?"

"Yes, very much so."

"Where then," Gerhard asked with a note of triumph in his vioce, "Do you think God has all this information stored, everything everybody has thought, said, and done?"

Fritz seemed perfectly unabashed. "I don't know. Why don't you ask Him?"

"Ask who?"

"Ask God."

"That's stupid. How can you ask somebody something when you don't even believe he exists?"

"How can you ring the doorbell when you don't believe someone lives in the house? You ring the bell, and if nothing happens, no one is there who wants to answer. If someone comes to the door, the conversation starts. If this business about God knowing all things troubles you, if you ask Him how it works and nothing happens, you have lost nothing. But let me warn you."

"Warn me about what?"

"Do not ask if you want to stay ignorant."

"Why would I want to stay ignorant?"

Fritz took another draw on his pipe and filled their corner of the room with smoke. "It's your excuse, Gerhard. As long as that question remains unanswered you don't have to open your mind or your life to the Lordship of Jesus Christ. You're hiding behind it."

Gerhard was incensed. "I hide from nothing."

"Then ask."

* * *

The meeting that night was much the same, but the topic under discussion was different. It was more to the point. Once again it was the question and answer time that got to Gerhard. Richter had talked about the necessity of the death of Christ for the forgiveness of sin and Gerhard had let it float over his head. He had no sin. It was as though the first questioner had read Gerhard's mind.

"Herr Richter, what do you say to someone who thinks they are not a sinner?"

Richter turned back to the black board and erased it. Then he wrote: 1, 2, 3, 4. "I ask such a man to take four pieces of paper and say to him, put a list of things on each page. On page 1, write down every time you can remember when you have said 'yes' and meant 'no' or said 'no' and meant 'yes.' Also write down everytime you can remember when you told an outright lie. Write down everytime you gave an employee a shady answer, every time you made a promise and broke it and every time you made a promise and never intended to keep it.

"On page 2," Rickter turned and wrote the second heading, "Write what it is that you hide from everybody. Be honest. I do not want to see the paper; you need never show it to anyone but to yourself. Write down something that, if I found out about it, something inside you would wither.

"On page 3," he turned and wrote again, "Make a list of friends to whom you have done something that you would not want them to do to you. Never mind whether or not they did something to provoke you, just put down your part."

He turned to the board for the last time. "On page 4 write the names of the people for whom you have done something good, and done it without hope of any compensation or reward of any kind. Things that were purely altruistic.

"I think that any man who does that honestly will see that he is a sinner and that he is desperately in the need of salvation. He will know, intuitively, that the sin and the wrong he has written down is only the tip of an iceberg."

Gerhard made notes in his own shorthand across a small piece of paper he had with him. He had the four headings. When the meeting broke up, he walked directly back to the clinic and into his room. It was comfortable enough, a good bed, an overstuffed chair and a desk with a desk chair. There was a large window that looked out on a garden, but the curtains were drawn—it was night. He seated himself and glanced at his copy of Goethe. A battle went on in his mind.

Why was he afraid to write? Why was he afraid to take a look at himself?

Better to get it over with and then forget it. He was a good man, a good father. What did he have to worry about?

He took four pieces of stationery out of the desk drawer and labeled them as Richter had suggested. Then he started writing. He was amazed and discomforted by how many things he could put on the first page, and then, by how many things he could put on the second. It was worse with the third. He had no idea he had done so many terrible things to so many people. But, it was the fourth page that got to him. It was blank.

When had he done anything for anybody without hope of any kind of a reward? True, he had gotten his family away from the Communists at great sacrifice, but it had been his family. He hadn't even helped his niece, he didn't want to endanger himself for ten seconds on her behalf. There was no one, absolutely no one, whom he could bring to mind for whom he had done anything genuinely unselfish.

Then it hit him. He knew suddenly where God stored data, he got an answer to his question without asking for an answer. Apparently God answered some prayers before they were prayed. God stored the data about Gerhard Dirks in Gerhard Dirks. Everything he had ever thought, seen, heard, said, done—everything was there and the data in his mind was unchangeable, unalterable and irrevocable. He was his own "file." Every human being was his own file. It was true that he could not recall everything, but that could be changed too. When that happened, he would be his own "readout." God didn't need to store data anywhere else.

Now he had lost both his excuses for not believing. Men do change—Fritz had changed, and there is information for a final judgement—every man carries his own data. He looked down at the papers in front of him and spoke to himself out loud.

"Gerhard Dirks, I don't think I like you."

Then he brought his fist down on the desk with a bang. "No, this is not fair. I am looking only at the things that are wrong; things are out of proportion."

Were they?

When a computer program is written, it is put into the computer and the programmer looks for errors. This is called "debugging." Gerhard realized that he was being "debugged."

He spoke out loud again. "How about the good things?"

There was a moment's silence and then once more he spoke. "When I put my program into a computer, I am not interested in what is right, that I ignore. What I want to know from the machine is, what is wrong? Gerhard, why do you think God is any different?"

Something inside of him broke and he let go of his right to his own life. The tears streamed down his face. He remembered the words from his catechism days. Sliding off his chair he got on his knees beside it and said, "Lord Jesus Christ, have mercy on me and wash me in your blood."

In a few minutes he stopped crying. He knew that something had happened. A wall had come down, the wall that had stood between him and his Creator. He hadn't known the wall was there, until it came down. It was the wall that Christ had demolished. Now, for the first time in his life, he knew what it meant to have fellowship with his Heavenly Father.

He thought of a better analogy. It wasn't a wall, it was more like a sphere made of stone—a sphere that formed a prison. It had kept him in, and God out.

It had kept others out too—out of his life and out of his heart. Just as he now knew his need for his Lord, so also something else awoke within him. He knew his need for fellowship with his brother.

He must find Fritz and tell him what had happened.

* * *

EPILOGUE

SAN FRANCISCO, CALIFORNIA. Dr. Gerhard Dirks, *now liberated from three imprisoning forces—Naziism, Communism, and atheism—describes his metamorphosis.*

"After I had yielded to Christ, I began a daily and serious study of the Gospels. Gradually, the person of Christ began to take shape in my mind. The Lord—so courageous and yet so tender. This is the kind of a person who makes life worth living. This is the kind of a person we should become. How our problems would decrease!

"My attitude toward others changed so. I had used people's weaknesses and mistakes, held such things over their heads to get out from them by fear what it was that I wanted. As God changed my heart, this changed. I began to see in people things to love. I began to see, also, that you can move people through love instead of through fear.

"Looking back at myself, before I knew the Lord—a hardheaded, stubborn, driving German business executive—I say, if God can do this for Gerhard Dirks, he can do it for anyone!"

A NOTE FROM THE

AUTHOR

I am aware that there is an apparent gap in this story. It is caused by the fact that I have tried to write this book, to the best of my ability, in a way that reflects what actually happened. It follows a real life.

When a writer produces a work of fiction, he can set the stage for the motivations and the subsequent actions of his characters. In fiction there can be and should be a reason for every action by every character. In real life, things are not so neatly arranged.

The conversion of Gerhard Dirks comes abruptly and without proper "plot" preparation. This is because that is what exactly happened.

Sometimes, God seems to say to some men in a clear and sudden way, "Come here." He said it to Gerhard Dirks and Gerhard Dirks came.

—C. Brandon Rimmer

APPENDIX

This is a copy of some of the material submitted to the Commissioner of Corporations, State of California. The information concerning Gerhard Dirks was submitted due to his participation in the formation of a corporation.

EDUCATION:

  April 1916-April 1929 Elementary/High School, Diploma
  April 1930-April 1934 Grad. School of Business, M.B.A.
      University of Leipzig Law School, Doctor of Laws

EXPERIENCE:

  April 1966-March 1968 IBM, Research, San Jose, Calif.,
      Management Consultant, Computer Development.
  April 1962-March 1966 IBM, Advanced Development
      Department, San Jose—Los Gatos, Calif., Management
      Consultant, Computer Development.
  April 1960-March 1962 IBM, Research, San Jose, Calif.,
      Management Consultant, Computer Development.
  March 1948-Dec. 1956 Association of German Machine
      Manufacturers, Frankfurt/Main, Germany, Department
      Head: Accounting and Industrial Organization, Cost
      studies, Factory visits and committee work. Committee
      members were officers of major German machine factories.
      Lecture tours through all major German cities for
      manufacturers of electromachines. Courses taught
      concerning inventory and production control for German
      manufacturers, sponsored by AWF (Committee for
      Economic Manufacturing).
  March 1950-Dec. 1956 Association of German Industry

(Bundesverband der Deutschen Industri, Loeln/Rhein). Unified accounting systems, Models for typical industries, cost accounting rules; Negotiation with Ministry of Economics for the re-evaluation of German assets after the war (WW II) and for the price rules for Defense and other public works.

March 1950-March 1960 Management consultant work for larger German corporations (Osram, Brown-Boveri, C. W. Freudenberg, etc.). Cost ratio comparisons in consumer-industry. (This work financed personal computer development experiments.)

June 1943-April 1945 Skodaserke AG, Prague. Line controller for all Skoda factories. 65,000 employees in steel mills, foundries, machinery, electro-machinery, cars, tanks, artillery, airplanes and locomotives, etc. 3,000,000 punched cards monthly; first German production control system using punched cards. Established standard accounting system for the plants.

July 1942-May 1943 Waffen-Union Skoda-Bruenn. Staff Controller; same functions as below.

Jan. 1940-June 1942 Reichswerke fuer Waffen-und Maschinebau Berlin. Staff controller, 240,000 employees. Corporate structure included Rheinmetall-Borsig, Skoda, Waffenwerke Brueen, Steyr-Caimler-Puch, etc. Transfer to Prague to Skoda-Waffenwerke Bruenn, successor to Reichwerke AG. fuer Waffen-und Maschinenebau after headquarters had been bombed out in Berlin.

July 1938-Dec. 1939 NG Studiengesellschaft, Berlin. Head of study group for the organization of accounting and production control of the departments of heavy machinery and electromachinery.

Jan. 1938-June 1938 Merceds-Bueromaschinen-Cmbh, Zella Mohlis. Manager of Organization-Department for Accounting-machines, Sales. Office Machine factory employing 4,500.

Dec. 1934-Dec. 1927 Heerbrandt A.G. Raguhn. Manager of Financial and Cost-Accounting Department. Machine factory.

Dec. 1933-Nov. 1934 Papierfabriken Muldenstein/Neidhardsthal, Leipzig. Assistant to General Manager of Cost-Accounting Department. Corporation of three paper and card-board mills.

INVENTIONS-PATENT RIGHTS:

European patent rights with a priority date before Jan. 1, 1958, and some others are not listed as they have been exclusively licensed and are no longer under Dirks' control. These early basic inventions for the whole computer industry include:

1943	Rotating magnetic memories (Drum, Disc)
	Magnetic digital tapes (Self-clocking bit recording)
	Magnetic stripes on ledger cards (Self-clocking bit recording)
	Magnetic strip magazine (Self-clocking bit recording)
1947/8	Rotating magnetic memories with track-selection by movable heads
	Start-stop magnetic digital tapes for sorting and transfer to matrix-storage
	Transfer from magnetic matrix storage into tapes, discs and printers
	Serial transfer from storage into matrix storage and parallel transfer into printers and display devices

LICENSE AGREEMENTS:

Oct. 1954	License Agreement with Siemag, Germany (renewed Dec. 1960)
April 1957	License Agreement with ICT, Great Britain (renewed May 1967)
July 1957	License Agreement with Zuse, Germany
Sept. 1959	License Agreement with ABM, Remington Rand, U.S.A.
June 1960	License Agreement with Bull, France

These license agreements were based mainly upon European patent rights. Until 1960 none of the U.S. patents had been issued. Since then, some U.S. patents have been issued with early priority dates. Some patent applications (U.S.) are still pending.

SELECTIVE SURVEY OF DIRKS-PATENTS ISSUED IN
UNITED STATES AND GREAT BRITAIN

SHORT-TITLE	PRIORITY	US-PATENT	GB-PATENT
ADDRESSABLE FILES AND MEMORIES			
Rotatable Magnetic Storage	GY 1948	3.228.007	786.033
Drum Files	GB 1955	3.049.694	827.163
Magnetic Start-Stop Data-Storage	GB 1957	3.213.437	824.227
Disc-File and Removable Disc-Pack	GB 1955	3.172.082	820.115
Tiltable/Shiftable Heads on Magn. Media	GB 1955		827.165

Addressing Cyclic Storage	GB 1956		824.227
Vernier Clock Generating Means	GB 1956	3.042.906	817.517
Electronic Storage Matrix (A)	GY 1948	3.205.483	786.028
Electronic Storage Matrix (B)	GY 1948	RE 26.032	786.028
Read Only Core-Memory	GY 1948	2.982.951	786.041

PRINTING AND DISPLAY DEVICES

Serial Reading into Parallel Printers	GY 1948	2.972.016	786.028
Serial Cyclic Storage into Printers	GY 1948	2.964.739	
Parallel Typewheel Printer	GB 1955	2.928.896	854.309
Line-Wise Image Printer	GY 1948	2.976.801	786.028
Matrix-Signals for Image-Printers	GB 1959	2.997.152	
Cathode-Ray Tube Display from Storage	GY 1948	4.027.287	786.036
Control of Successive Key Movements	GB 1956		821.047
Text-Composition Printing	GY 1948	3.063.536	786.037
Text Justification	GY 1948	2.971.626	786.038
Stroboscopic Indication	GY 1948	3.056.955	786.028

SELECTIVE DATA-TRANSFERS BETWEEN TAPES/FILES/MEMORIES

Parallel Track Stepwise Tapes	GY 1948	3.042.901	786.034
Selective Writing on Tape	GY 1948	2.967.295	786.029
Crosswise Recording on Tape	GB 1957	2.986.725	858.766
Two-Tape Sorting	GY 1948	2.928.077	786.031
Plural-Tape Sorting	GY 1948	3.094.684	786.030
Improved Tape Sorting	GB 1956		823.782
Presensing with Selective Transfer	GB 1956	2.972.131	817.596
Group-Controlled Selective Transfer	GB 1956		827.310
Dynamic Sorting Tape/Discs	GB 1959	3.242.466	958.831
Data-Transfer Shiftg/Zeroising	GB 1957	3.088.102	851.752
Counter Controlled Data-Transfer	GB 1958	3.037.194	879.295
Selective Data-Transfer	GB 1959	3.102.997	886.352
Inverse Track Recording	GB 1957	3.281.804	846.493
Signal-Transfer with Group-Markers	GB 1956		818.253
Data Transm with Autom. Repit. on Errors	GB 1955	3.001.017	853.691
Data Handling System	US 1963	3.343.133	1102.714

SHEET STORAGE DEVICES

Magnetic Sheet Mass-Storage	GB 1957		862.122
Magnetic Sheet Magazine Storage	GB 1955		823.495
Magnetic Ledger Card Apparatus	GY 1948	3.031.647	786.029
Applying Magnetic Stripes on Carriers	GB 1954	2.997.417	818.465
Envelops with Magnetic Stripes	GB 1956		818.465

Mark-Sensing of Serialized Data	GB 1956		817.902
Machine Readable Optical Markings	GB 1957		844.215
Counter Controlled Line-Selection	GB 1956		818.078
Index Storage	GB 1956		816.623

ARITHMETIC UNITS

Serial Decimal Adder	GY 1948	2.931.572	786.048
Adders for Interlaced Pulse-Trains	GB 1957	3.018.960	837.196
Multiplying with Pulse-Trains	GB 1955		852.184
Distribut. Computing Means	GB 1955		837.197
Small Electronic Computing Means	GB 1955	3.022.950	852.182

CARD READERS

Parallel Card-Readers	GY 1948	3.029.020	786.025
Serial Card-Reader	GB 1957	3.060.414	

TEXT COMPOSING DEVICES

Line Composing Recorder	GB 1955	3.106.336	852.152
AC Tape Perforator	US 1963	3.093.303	1012768
Keyboard Control for Line-Comp. Machines	GB 1956	3.223.979	875.012
Matrix Control Line-Comp Keyboard	GB 1956		875.013
Signal Controlled Time-Delay	GB 1956	3.010.095	822.312
Text-Correcting Perforator	GB 1956	3.011.154	837.111

DEVICES FOR THE ELECTRONIC CONTROL OF MECHANICAL DEVICES

Step-Wisely Controlled Electr. Motor	GB 1956		825.756
Electronic Counter Clutch Control	GB 1956	2.971.623	855.953

This survey refers only to patents issued in USA and GB.
It does not include Dirks-Patents or -applications in Germany (some of them dating back to 1942) or
other countries in Europe (Belgium, France, Italy, Switzerland), in America (Argentina, Brazil, Canada) and in South Africa, India and Australia.